RECOVER YOUR PERSPECTIVE

A GUIDE TO UNDERSTANDING YOUR EATING
DISORDER AND CREATING RECOVERY USING
CBT, DBT, AND ACT

JANEAN ANDERSON, PH.D., CEDS

POPLAR PRESS

Recover Your Perspective: A Guide to Understanding Your Eating Disorder and Creating Recovery Using CBT, DBT, and ACT

Janean Anderson, Ph.D., CEDS

Newsletter sign-up at www.DrJaneanAnderson.com

This book is for my clients who have taught me more than they know, for the dedicated professionals tirelessly working to end eating disorders, and for everyone brave enough to choose recovery.

CONTENTS

PART I

An Introduction to Recovering Your Perspective

"The beginning of wisdom is the definition of terms."
                                        - Socrates

1

INTRODUCTION

When I had an eating disorder, I thought I would never get better. Years ago, in the thick of my struggles, my world was madness and misery. My truest, most constant emotion was hopelessness. Whole days were consumed with worries about my weight, tracking calories, and merciless self-criticism. My eating disorder was my everything; I genuinely believed recovery was not possible, that I would never get better.

But, here's the thing: I *did* get better.

If we rewound my life back to early adolescence, you'd see a girl in a most delicate position, trying to successfully navigate innumerable concerns at school and at home, all while accumulating tiny breadcrumbs of information that I'd use to form my opinion of myself. You'd also see the first bloom of my eating disorder. Anorexia laid down deep roots and thrived because of all the ways the circumstances of my life watered it. You see, life will always give you reasons to use your eating disorder, always give you reasons to feel you are not enough.

Years passed slowly, miserably, marked by peaks and depressions of both hope and eating disorder behaviors. It was a long, rough, soul-deadening experience to live life with an eating disorder. When I finally got honest and committed to the real work of recovery, everything changed.

Everything changed really fucking slowly. It was infuriating. I learned I'd become so close to my eating disorder that I thought the two were one and the same. It took me years to stop using all eating disorder behaviors, and longer still to repair the eating disorder thoughts, gently sweeping them away until my mind was clean again, until my mind was my own.

Arguably the best thing that has ever happened in my life is my own recovery. It's not only about me. I wholeheartedly believe you can get better too. And I want to help you do it!

I have the unique and blessed experience of having my own recovery story while also (now) being a psychologist who gets to treat eating disorders. I chose to write that sentence that way. I *get* to treat eating disorders. I *get* to help people to do the hard, wondrous, magnificent work of recovery. I *get* to. What an honor. What an absolute honor.

I am lucky enough to have both perspectives. I understand eating disorders from the point of view of having lived with one and lived through the recovery process. I also understand eating disorders as a psychologist who treats them. As a psychologist, I now have the names for all the sneaky tricks eating disorders use and the twisted thought patterns they produce. I can identify exactly what the eating disorder is doing when one of my clients is talking about their struggles. Now, I want to teach you these same concepts.

The first concept is this: You are not your eating disorder. I repeat, you are NOT your eating disorder. Though I'm well aware they can very much feel the same, one of the most important things you can do in your recovery is to separate yourself from your eating disorder. Specifically, it is critical to separate *your* thoughts from your eating disorder's thoughts.

The fundamental problem is that having an eating disorder causes you to lose perspective, the perspective of your true self, who you really are. When you have an eating disorder, you are too close to the problem to see the way out; you can't see the proverbial forest through the trees. The eating disorder and all the rest of your thoughts feel equally true. You're used to thinking them all the time; they feel like a normal part of your thought process but the truth is, they're not. Some of these thoughts are solely the product of the disorder itself.

That's right. Your eating disorder has its own thoughts. I don't mean to say you literally hear another voice, different from your own internal dialogue. What I'm referring to are the specific thought patterns resulting only from your eating disorder. If you didn't have that disorder, you wouldn't be having those thoughts.

For example, you might wake up, step on the scale (again), see the number and think to yourself: "Ahhhh, I can't believe this! I'm disgusting. I'll have to restrict today to make up for it." It seems like *you* thought that thought but in reality, *that was your eating disorder talking*, not you. It's not likely your authentic self would be so harsh, so unreasonable, and so condemning let alone lead you to the decision to reduce your caloric intake, potentially harming your health, all because of a number on a scale.

It's okay; there's no need to judge yourself for this

because that was your eating disorder thinking, not you. This book emphasizes the principle that separating your thoughts and actions from those generated by your eating disorder will lead you to recovery, living as your authentic self.

I want to emphasize that it's not the thought itself necessarily, but more the thought in context. Sure, you might think: "I hate my body today. It's fat." Thinking that way doesn't mean you have an eating disorder. However, if you do have an eating disorder, those thoughts are part of a cycle, a buildup toward using eating disorder behaviors and that's why it's important to look at your thoughts. Again, it's important to consider the context in which your thoughts occur.

I also want to acknowledge that everyone thinks about the authentic self differently. When I was trained, "authentic self" referred to the truest, core parts of someone's being. To me, my authentic self is who I am when I don't perform or impress, and when I live in accordance with my values. Others might call this their "ideal self." Some might say every moment you experience is technically your authentic self because you can't be anyone else.

I don't care how you choose to think about it; I just care that you feel better. Think about it in whatever way is most helpful, without judgment and with lots of curiosity and compassion.

You can leverage the power of three of the most effective therapy methods, not only to help identify eating disorder thought patterns but also to take action toward your recovery. These methods are Cognitive Behavioral Therapy (CBT), Dialectical Behavior Therapy (DBT), and Acceptance and Commitment Therapy (ACT).

This book will distill the keystone ideas from these

complex therapeutic frameworks and make them easy to understand. You can then use these remarkable therapies' key concepts in the context of your eating disorder, helping you understand the underlying psychological processes happening in yourself, giving you tools you can implement in your recovery.

THE BIRTH OF THIS BOOK

This book grew out of my years of work in individual and group therapy in clinical settings, with my many clients who have eating disorders. Day after day, year after year—no matter what setting I practiced in, where I worked or with whom—whenever I worked with people who had eating disorders, I heard the same statements over and over. I noticed common threads and heard the same eating disorder thoughts uttered out loud.

Having an eating disorder brings with it a very specific, recognizable set of thoughts. These eating disorder thoughts can be thought of as patterns; they follow a relatively similar formula and have many common traits, new iterations of the same old thoughts you've been wrestling with for a great while. Again, it's okay and certainly not necessary to judge yourself for this; it's simply how eating disorders work.

In my clinical work, I listened to my clients speaking their eating-disordered thoughts and I, being a psychologist, would identify what those thoughts were using the training I'd received. For example, when one of my lovely, college-aged clients shared that she binged over the past weekend and stated, "…And I feel like after this weekend, I'll never be able to get my binging under control," I knew she was catastrophizing. That's when you assume the most catastrophic outcome will happen; you know, you're taking something minor and assuming the most catastrophic outcome possible is destined to result.

Catastrophizing will be described in much greater detail later and describes what is called a "cognitive distortion," meaning that our thinking is not aligned with reality. I absolutely understand how my client could think (and feel very real fear) that she'd never be able to stop her bingeing, but it's simply not true. Catastrophizing causes people to think of the absolute, worst-case scenario. *I binged this weekend, therefore, I will never, ever, ever be able to rid myself of bingeing. Ever.*

Untrue. The only reason you're thinking this is because of your eating disorder. This is how eating disorders work! They prey upon your most vulnerable thoughts, causing you to fall into cognitive (thought) pitfalls.

Think of it like this: You are walking along a path. Try to picture it; it winds through the woods and is twisting, muddy, rocky. Knotted roots are bulging out of the dirt. You can't see the entirety of the path or the endpoint as you walk along it. This path is recovery.

Unfortunately, you have the worst companion ever walking along this path with you; it's your eating disorder voice—the eating disorder thoughts. While you walk the path of recovery, your eating disorder thoughts are holding your hand, distracting you from paying attention to the path and walking you across ditches you fall into. And—the falling sucks. In fact, your falling can hurt so much you don't want to dig yourself out of the pit, dust yourself off, and keep walking your recovery path. This book will identify all the sneaky ways your eating disorder will distort your thoughts and try to steer you into thought pits, so you'll continue to use your eating disorder.

In a way, it's almost like having the playbook for a team you play against frequently, that always beats you. You go into the game with best intentions, play your hardest—blood, sweat, and tears ensue—only to lose to a surprise play you weren't expecting. Somehow, though you were present and fighting as valiantly as you could, you were taken by surprise, only to return to the familiar feeling of defeat the eating disorder so deftly lays at your feet each time.

Somehow, that binge episode came out of the blue. Somehow, though you had your meal plan outlined for the day, you were unable to follow it. Somehow, your best intention to resist the urge to purge wasn't strong enough to overpower the overwhelming need to use your eating disorder. Your eating disorder has you beat because you don't know what the play is. You don't know the name and how the play works, enabling it to sneak its way to victory. Don't judge yourself for this. It's not your fault. You were set up.

But a playbook outlines all the planned moves, all the common strategies a team uses. Having a list of the moves your rival team plans to use on you would be revolutionary, and that's exactly what you have in this book. This playbook will review the most common moves your eating disorder will use to keep you stuck. When you know what the eating disorder is likely to do, you can plan ahead, making your own recovery playbook instead of feeling bested each time.

HOW TO READ THIS BOOK

Before you dive into the content and concepts, I thought I would provide a little guidance for reading this book. Information follows on how to use the terms in the book and how to maintain a compassionate, non-judgmental stance while reading.

There Is Power In A Name

THE WORD "LABELING" has gotten a bad reputation as of late and, in many cases, rightfully so. No one wants to be "labeled." No one wants their complex human experiences to be minimized, boiled down, simplified. No eating disorder can be described in one word. No person can be described in one word, either.

That is not the intention of this book. As you start to look at the various thought patterns found in eating disorders, you'll see I'm not setting out to trivialize anyone's experiences, invalidate feelings, or stigmatize struggles. Instead, my intent is to help you empower yourself by increasing your understanding of the processes at hand.

What This Book Can Do...And What It Can't

THIS BOOK IS a guide introducing you to the basic principles of the three leading eating disorder therapies. You'll read descriptions of these concepts using examples from actual clients and, to the best of my ability, I've provided relatable, clear examples and information about clinical concepts. These should be both memorable and useful to you in your recovery, so I encourage you to take what you read into your therapy sessions, for further discussion.

By reading this book, you'll have a wealth of information to draw upon in your recovery including new terms, understanding of psychological processes, and suggestions for taking recovery-oriented action. You'll read about each of the therapeutic systems, CBT, DBT, and, ACT, learning the cornerstone concepts of each. With these, you'll develop new insight into your thoughts, feelings, and behaviors.

Each of these therapeutic approaches—CBT, DBT, and ACT—is a massive, comprehensive, impressive, dynamic, renowned approach. The approaches were each developed over many years by leaders in the field of psychology, and they're backed by the best research in the field, demonstrating their effectiveness.

CBT (Cognitive Behavioral Therapy) emphasizes how to change unhelpful thought patterns and behaviors. DBT (Dialectical Behavioral Therapy) encourages both acceptance of self and change of ineffective patterns, integrating two seemingly opposite goals. ACT (Acceptance and

Commitment Therapy) promotes identifying your values and taking committed action toward living them.

In sum, as CBT, DBT, and, ACT form three of the leading therapeutic approaches to date, there's no way they can be completely summarized, nor can every possible thought pattern be listed. This book cannot cover all possible scenarios and struggles, and that's not the intention; I simply hope to give you a strong foundation to build upon in working toward your recovery.

Judgement-Free Reading

MICHAEL J. Fox was once quoted as saying, "The least amount of judging we can do, the better off we are." The least amount of judging we can do, the better off we are, indeed! This applies to judging ourselves as well.

One thing about people who have eating disorders is that they tend to excel at judging themselves. Harshly. The problem with judging yourself harshly, aside from the fact that it feels awful, is that it's not helpful. When you judge yourself, you create negative feelings about yourself that get in the way of you receiving the feedback you need for recovery.

For example, your dietitian might tell you, "This week, you'll need to increase the [insert challenging food group here] in your meal plan. It looks like you didn't get enough over the past week." It would be easy to judge yourself. "Oh man, I failed. I didn't complete my meal plan this week. I could have done more. I'm terrible at following my meal plan." The reality is, you needed to add more of that food into your diet. It's not an indictment, it's just a fact. You'll find a great deal of empowerment when you're able to see things for what they are, and as the feedback you need rather than creating judgments and negative emotions that only block and distract you from fully absorbing the messages.

I can personally relate to beating myself up. I struggled to be gentle with myself; eventually, I needed to practice speaking kindly to myself until kindness and self-compassion became my default. Ultimately, kind self-talk replaced the unhelpful, harsh thoughts.

It can be easy to fault yourself for things you've done, things that have passed, perhaps even things you regret with your eating disorder. I encourage you to *practice* being kind instead of judging, both while you read this book and in your life as a whole.

THE RECOVERED SELF: YOUR AUTHENTIC SELF

The authentic self has been described in diverse ways by many authors, clinicians, and researchers alike. Your authentic self is who you really are. It's who you are under all the stuff you think you should be, are striving to be, and at times, are pretending to be. Your authentic self is buried underneath your eating disorder.

Let's dig.

Eating disorders are so powerful and pervasive they can feel like they *are* you. And, as I've said before, they are *not*. No one is born with an eating disorder; they develop along the way, cropping up from all kinds of sources for all kinds of reasons. But someone with an eating disorder is never who they start out as.

People don't start out life obsessed with diets, though sadly there's evidence that people are thinking about dieting at younger and younger ages. When we were kids, we cared about our health. We cared if we were too sick to play. We cared if we were too hungry to go play sports, and we cared if we were too tired to make forts and have fun. And that was authentic.

When we were younger, before eating disorders got their hooks in us, we liked a lot of things about ourselves. We liked being the funny kid in class. We liked being the sweet, considerate one. We cared when others around us were hurting. And that was authentic too. Even if you can't recall a time when you authentically liked yourself, you also know there was a time before your eating disorder became your focus.

But when an eating disorder takes over your life, your thoughts are beholden to it. You no longer worry about things you truly value and only care about what your eating disorder cares about. When the eating disorder takes over, all your behaviors revolve around what it wants you to do. You don't care about getting satisfaction and nourishment from your food; you only care about calories and about using eating disorder behaviors.

You don't feel like yourself. And, no wonder you don't. You're not thinking like yourself or acting like yourself. But, remember back to before you had an eating disorder; there were qualities you liked about yourself, qualities that felt true. When you were able to express them, you felt like yourself. You felt like *your authentic self*.

Living as your authentic self is a direct threat to your eating disorder. Eating disorders value secrecy and try to make you save face, telling you to cover up your "flaws," hide your struggles and never reach out to others for support.

Everything you do as your authentic self is going to contradict the eating disorder and foster recovery. If you shared and asked for help, it would make recovery a little easier. If you honored your health, it would take you further into recovery. If you're in touch with the strengths you have under the eating disorder, you'll realize you don't need that eating disorder to get through this life.

The solution is to reclaim your perspective. Recovery requires separating your eating disorder thoughts and behaviors from your authentic ones, from your authentic self. Sometimes, people are so fused, so stuck in their eating disorder that they cannot see which thoughts are truly theirs and which are the result of the disorder.

This book systematically outlines these patterns using the most effective eating disorder therapies: Cognitive Behavioral Therapy (CBT), Dialectical Behavioral Therapy (DBT), and Acceptance and Commitment Therapy (ACT). Only by identifying these thought patterns for what they are, calling spades "spades," can you take the power away from the eating disorder and make choices for your authentic self. This is the essence of recovery and this is what it means to recover your perspective.

Imagine what's hiding under your eating disorder. I bet underneath all that pressure, under all the food rules, under all the counting, is someone extraordinary.

EATING DISORDER LIES

Eating disorders tell lies. This is a difficult truth you'll grapple with throughout your journey in recovery. When you have an eating disorder, the thought pattern, the way of thinking that comes with it, subtly and not-so-subtly feeds you lies. Distortions, too, are lies.

These lies are big and small, obvious and insidious, all ultimately designed to pull you deeper into the disorder. The lies are the eating disorder telling you to misstep on the path of recovery, tricking you into falling into a pit of distortions.

Lies exist in many forms. The first is the obvious eating disorder lie. These are untruths so plainly false they'd almost be laughable if the eating disorder didn't back them with massive amounts of fear. Here's an obvious eating disorder lie: "If I'm not a size [insert magical, life-changing pant size here], then I'll never find someone to be with and will die alone. In a box. On the street. In the cold."

You might read that sentence and notice how it feels extreme, bordering on melodramatic. You might also read it and feel the all-too-real fear of possibly ending up alone. I deeply empathize with both readings, and herein lies the delicate dance of recovery through recovering your perspective; you're validating how profoundly fearful your eating disorder tricks you into feeling while challenging the absurdity of its lie.

Another form of the lie is the twist. The twist contains a kernel of truth but your eating disorder takes that kernel and reshapes it into a different form to serve its own purposes. The twist can be thought of as the truth getting lost in translation because, let's face it, eating disorders are terrible at interpreting reality.

A twist might look something like this: Your boss tells you your new, wide-leg trousers look great on you. The truth is simply that... your boss thinks your new, wide-leg trousers look great on you! No hidden agenda. Not a backhanded compliment.

But then, your eating disorder takes the truth and twists, interpreting the compliment its own way. "Great, my boss thinks I look good because these wide-leg trousers are the only cut that can fit my fat legs. And my fat butt. Hell, I should probably just give up on pants altogether because I can't even fit into skinny pants. Ugh, I feel awful. I can't believe she said that. What a bitch."

Do you see in that example how the simple complimentary truth became completely warped into an entirely different message than was intended? The only reason it was twisted was because of the eating disorder lying to you.

The final form of eating disorder lie is denial. Denial takes many forms from flat-out refusal to acknowledge the truth, to sly minimization. Omission and ignoring parts of the story or the information you need are also forms of denial, and denial blocks you from fully dealing with the problem. If you don't acknowledge the severity of the problem, you can't create a solution equal in power to match your recovery needs.

An example I use with clients is to think about the eating disorder as a tumor. If you had a cancerous tumor growing in your gut, you'd want to know how big it was, how far it had spread, how good or bad the situation, even if that truth was hard to hear. When you have an eating disorder, it's like having a tumor in your gut.

If your doctor told you that you had a 10-pound tumor in your gut, you'd feel devastated by the news and you'd prepare to treat the entire tumor, no matter how awful the treatment was going to be. You'd want the tumor completely gone, forever. But when you have an eating disorder, it's like having a 10-pound tumor that you insist is only half a pound.

Your treatment team may have even told you this is a 10-pound tumor but you insist it's only half a pound and, subsequently, only engage in treatment for half a pound's worth of tumor, with the same low level of dedication to the process.

This is how the eating disorder uses denial to lie to you. The eating disorder is incredibly adept at making you ignore red flags, downplay warning signs, and completely deny outright things that don't serve the disorder's purpose of self-perpetuating, of keeping itself going.

Take comfort in the fact none of these lies are your fault. They happen in all eating disorders, all the time. It is your responsibility to recover your perspective and take down the walls of denial, brick by brick. That's where your power lies. You can recover only when you can be truly honest with yourself.

Through my years of clinical experience working with

people in therapy for eating disorders, I noticed that eating disorders not only lied in the same predictable ways (obvious lies, twists, and denial) but that they also lied about all the same things. Comprehensively summarizing all the things eating disorders lie to people about is beyond what any human being can do. However, I've identified four common categories of lies the eating disorder focuses on. These categories will appear in every section of the book, enabling you to see how the eating disorder is lying to you in your life. The categories are as follows:

- Lies about Food
- Lies about Self
- Lies about Others
- Lies about Treatment

You may find yourself wondering why I haven't discussed body image more. Perhaps body image is inextricably tied to eating-disordered behaviors for you, but choosing to write about food and leaving out a section on body or body image was intentional. I chose not to discuss body image as its own section and, instead, to incorporate it into other sections where it felt relevant because body image is not necessarily a part of someone's eating disorder.

My understanding of eating disorders is that although body image *can* be a critical piece in the development and maintenance of an eating disorder, it is not for everyone. A more universal, comprehensive view of the functions of eating disorders is that they are commonly used to regulate emotions, and emotion regulation is a broader, more inclusive understanding of one of the core functions of eating disorders. Of course, eating disorders are multi-faceted, layered, complex disorders that cannot be summarized easily and need to be understood within the individual's unique context. Anything else seems reductionistic.

PART II

Understanding Your Eating Disorder Using CBT

Cognitive Behavioral Therapy

"Thought is action in rehearsal."
-Sigmund Freud

HOW CBT WORKS

CBT stands for Cognitive Behavioral Therapy (sometimes written as Cognitive-Behavioral), the combination of cognitive therapy and behavioral therapy. In cognitive therapy, unhelpful and negative thoughts are "reframed"—thought of in a different way—and are identified and challenged. Behavioral therapy has clients identify what behaviors—the actual things they do in day to day life—are unhelpful, and the client and therapist collaboratively generate a plan to change that unhelpful behavior. In CBT, therefore, both thoughts *and* behaviors are addressed and improved.

The central thesis of CBT is that thoughts, behaviors, and feelings are inextricably linked and interact with one another. CBT aims to change unhelpful thoughts and behavior, resulting in feeling more positive emotions and increased psychological wellbeing.

CBT is a solution-focused form of therapy, meaning that it aims to create measurable change in your life, often in the quickest way possible for your present concern. CBT was developed by Dr. Aaron Beck in the 1960s and to this day remains one of the most effective and widely researched types of therapy; research shows it's helpful in treating depression, anxiety, chronic pain, substance abuse, and eating disorders.[1]

CBT is also one of the most prolific, well-respected forms of therapy. In fact, it is so expansive that other therapies, such as DBT—which will be explored later in the book —fall under the broad umbrella of cognitive behavioral therapies. Summarizing the origins, research, and clinical applications of CBT over the past 50 years is beyond the scope of this book, but if you'd like to learn more, please visit the website for The Beck Institute for Cognitive-Behavioral Therapy at www.BeckInstitute.org.

One of the primary ways CBT helps clients to create change is by identifying unhelpful thoughts, called cognitive distortions, and by challenging them or changing them altogether. In the following chapters, we'll explore how you can use concepts from CBT to help challenge and change your own unhelpful thoughts and prevent unhelpful eating disorder behaviors, resulting in experiencing positive emotions more frequently. Each chapter in the CBT section of the book will present a specific cognitive distortion to examine.

Problematic Eating Disorder Patterns Explained Using CBT: Cognitive Distortions

Cognitive distortions are inaccurate thought patterns. The following sections review specific types of cognitive distortions, showing you how eating disorders change your thoughts.

ALL-OR-NONE THINKING

"All-or-none" thinking, also called "black and white think-ing," is characterized by the lack of gray, of nuance, and of flexibility of thoughts. With all-or-none thinking, things are divided into absolutes and extremes. Either you're perfect or you're terrible. Either you're kicking ass in recovery or you've made no progress. Either you eat healthy foods or you're on a fast food binge bender. Either you get all A's in your classes or you're a failure. Any of this sound familiar? I have a hunch that it does.

All-or-none thinking is one of the most common cogni-tive distortions found in eating disorders; by its nature, it doesn't allow for flexibility, creativity, or forgiveness. With all-or-none thinking, the eating disorder pigeonholes you into a hopeless conundrum that's near impossible to work your way out of.

Instead of dropping the all-or-none thinking, most people align themselves with the more positive or socially desirable side of its polarized options. You may choose to try to get all A's because, with all-or-none thinking, the only other option is to consider yourself a failure.

All-or-none thinking is a great way to drive yourself into complete frustration, misery, and anxiety. What's more is that all-or-none thinking will make you feel utterly stuck, and *frequently*. Why? Because recovery, and well, life, aren't clean cut enough to fit into all-or-none, black and white boxes. Beyond this, people with eating disorders often use all-or-none thinking to draw conclusions about themselves.

You might wonder: Am I beautiful? Am I a good student? Am I a good friend? Am I worthy?

All-or-none thinking is a dangerous trap because everyone can think of times when they didn't feel beautiful, weren't good students, weren't good friends or felt unworthy. All-or-none thinking doesn't allow for exceptions. And there are always exceptions. People generally thought of as good, caring, kindhearted, loyal friends also have bad days or bad interactions, or bad months where they're less than the all-too-elusive mythical creature we'll call "perfect." P.S. Perfect doesn't exist. It's like Sasquatch or the Loch Ness Monster. People think they've seen it but there's no proof of it. It's a myth.

However, since all-or-none thinking only operates in extremes, and our mythical, magical unicorn of a concept called perfection is an extreme itself, it's one of the *two* options you can pursue. Only two. The other option is you can feel like a piece of shit about yourself if perfection doesn't work out for you. Some choice, huh?

In my life, I've definitely fallen victim to all-or-none thinking. I was certainly beholden to all-or-none thinking while in the depths of my eating disorder. All-or-none thinking showed up in every aspect of my life. No domain was safe. No area was good enough, protected from it. Every arena from being a student to being a daughter, to being someone's girlfriend and even my food and exercise patterns were subjected to the brutality of all-or-none thinking.

As a student, I always pushed myself to get all A's. I come from a family where academic achievement is praised and prized, so naturally, I wanted to reap the rewards. I wanted to feel successful. I wanted to feel lovable. I wanted to be proud of myself.

All-or-none thinking had me fooled. I was fooled into thinking if I got all A's, my feelings about myself would change, and that I'd actually have some semblance of self-esteem. All-or-none thinking makes big promises. The positive side of all-or-none thinking, the one that promises a glorious extreme (e.g. being perfect, impenetrable self-esteem, loved by all) is incredibly seductive. The problem is that it never delivers.

Though most of the time I did make A's in school, inevitably there were times I did not. Now, looking back after 10 years in recovery, I see there was no way I could have possibly made all A's all the time. My all-or-none thinking was so extreme that if I couldn't get 100% on whatever I was working on, I didn't get the ultimate prize of self-esteem. Every time I'd score anything less than 100%—which, by the way, is 99% of all other possible scores—I'd immediately emotionally spiral out of control. I'd plummet downward toward the other end of the continuum of the all-or-none setup, beginning to feel like an absolute failure. If I didn't get 100%, all my efforts were worthless and so was I. I'd score something wonderful like 92% and think, "What a freakin' waste! I studied so hard for nothing! Why couldn't I just get a perfect score?" I'm sure you can think of an example from your own life where you engaged in all-or-nothing thinking, a time when you either did things perfectly or all was lost.

The reason why eating disorders love to operate in all-or-none, black or white thinking is because it has a profound capacity to make you feel terrible about yourself and the things you do. What's even more twisted is that the eating disorder can make you feel awful about the way you're doing your eating disorder itself! All-or-none thinking leads you to feel you didn't even do your eating disorder well enough; you didn't restrict enough, work out enough, count calories accurately enough. The list goes on.

Your eating disorder can even use all-or-none thinking to make you feel not good enough, inadequate in your recovery. I can't tell you how many times I've heard my clients say, "I feel like I'm failing at recovery. I messed up one meal in my meal plan." It makes me think, by that standard, who *is* doing well enough in recovery?

By now, you probably see all-or-none thinking is a complete, no-win trap. Having an eating disorder, creating your recovery, and generally living life as a human being on planet earth necessitates the ability to understand nuance, to be flexible, and to live in the gray spaces where life isn't so straightforward. Your eating disorder applies all-or-none thinking to the four primary categories we're examining in this book, the first of which is food. Let's start there.

Food

YOUR EATING DISORDER needs you to think of food in black and white terms. This kills flexibility, understanding, and quite honestly, also kills a lot of the fun of eating. The more miserable you are and the worse off you feel about yourself, the more likely you are to use eating disorder behaviors.

Remember, the main mission of your eating disorder is to keep itself going.

One of the most obvious examples of how eating disorders use all-or-none thinking is by having you think of food in terms of "good foods" and "bad foods." Heads-up, people: food doesn't have inherent qualities of good or evil. It's just food.

All-or-none thinking results in thoughts such as, "Carbs are bad," "Fats make you fat," "Sugar is the enemy," "Veggies are okay to eat," "I can only eat the foods on my good list," "Eating clean is better," and "This food is healthy, that food isn't."

Good calorie, bad calorie, all-or-none, dichotomous thinking is what makes it possible for people with eating disorders to create "good" or "bad" food lists in the first place. If you're operating with all-or-none rules, you are trapped. Inevitably, you will eat foods off the "bad list" and you'll also have days where you don't adhere to the "good list" to your eating disorder's satisfaction. Then, you get to feel bad about breaking the rules and subsequently use eating disorder behaviors to deal with feelings of disappointment, frustration, and failure.

A truly vicious cycle.

I encourage you to take some time to think of ways all-or-none thinking shows up in your relationship with food, what food rules you have.

Self

ALL-OR-NONE THINKING CAN RESULT in stark, absolute conclusions about ourselves such as, "I over-ate again! I told myself I wasn't going to. I've failed." The condemning conclusions about ourselves seem endless. Remember, all-or-none thinking only gives you two possible options: 1) Succeed perfectly every single time or, 2) toss out all the good pieces of evidence about who you are and feel miserable and lowly instead.

Herein lies a major problem: no one does things perfectly every single time. No one ever has. No one ever will. Trust me, if you're reading this book you're probably the type of person who's tried with all possible human force to meet those standards. If anyone could have made it happen, it would have been you. But it hasn't because *it's not possible.*

Moreover, you're up against life. Life hands everyone failures not because *they* are failures but because failures are natural; life gives out failures to everyone. At the risk of sounding insensitive, I'd like to ask you this (and please read this with my very kindest, warmest, softest voice in your mind): what makes you so different and special that you're not allowed to fail?

People need to fail in order to grow. How did your eating disorder get you to the point where failure, which is necessary, inevitable, and can be one of the deepest gifts life can give us, became off-limits for you? All-or-none thinking puts a crushing weight and immense pressure on you to accomplish—and I chose that word "accomplish" with purpose—what no other human being has ever done: perfect behavior at all times.

All-or-none thinking shuns failure. You're either successful or you're not. You succeeded or you failed. This way of thinking stands in stark contrast to nuance which would say, "I succeeded and failed, and the scale of my failures and successes depends on the angle at which I look into the reflecting glass."

Sadder still is that all-or-none thinking about yourself works like a moving target. As you continue to live life, experiencing successes and failures and everything that exists in between, the target moves. The target itself is like a dartboard, except that inner circle with the greatest rewards is a mere fraction of how large the already-small circle is. It is impossible to hit. The target represents doing everything right all the time.

This is part of how all-or-none thinking works. The only feel-good-about-yourself option is impossible to stick the dart on. The stakes are incredibly high in this scenario because that teeny, tiny part of the target you need to hit comes with an incredible prize, the prize of self-esteem. Even if it's fleeting, feeling good about yourself is a potent drug. With all-or-none thinking, this can only be a quick high wherein you're tricked into believing you've met these high standards, only to discover later that the ephemeral high has long since passed and the target has moved again. The target is still there if you'd like to continue with your dart throwing at the tiny, impossible circle. To me, this sounds exhausting.

Having horrendously low self-esteem is exhausting too. I can attest to how truly tiring all-or-none thinking and the subsequent absence of self-esteem can be. Looking back into my eating disorder days, or as I sometimes jokingly call them, The Dark Days, I can call to mind my complete and utter obsession with wanting people to like me.

To give you a better sense of how intense and irrational this fixation was, think of the most enthralling show you've ever binge-watched, hour after hour, on Netflix. Think of the feeling you had when Netflix prompted you to continue watching even though you'd been glued to it for hours and knew it wasn't good for you. You couldn't pull yourself away, could you? And that's how it is; you just can't pull back.

I felt about people liking me just the same as I felt in those moments when I couldn't rip myself away from glorious video streaming; I was swallowed whole with no hope of pulling myself out. Unfortunately for me, my eating disorder commandeered my priorities and threw me directly into the tractor beam of wanting all people to like me. And, if we're really being honest, I'm saying I wanted them to *really* like me.

The eating disorder ever so wisely paired this deep desire for acceptance, love, and belonging (that depended on other adolescents' opinions of me!) with the absolute trap of all-or-none thinking. You see, it wasn't enough for my eating disorder to have people like me, even *really* like me; no, my eating disorder required that *everyone* would like me. All people liked me or I felt like no one liked me. Everyone, or no one counted. All or none. Black or white. Completely dichotomous without any gray. And then I would restrict until I fainted, to punish myself for not being able to win the hearts of other finicky, angsty teens. The vicious cycle of the eating disorder carried on with the support of its sponsor, all-or-nothing thinking.

Others

ALL-OR-NONE THINKING HAS ALSO PROUDLY SPONSORED some cruel messages about others. Your eating disorder engages in all-or-none thinking about others to send you into complete emotional turmoil and ultimately, you'll use more behaviors. Your eating disorder keeps itself going by distorting your perception of others and your expectations of how other people will treat you. This is wildly problematic.

I'm sure you've heard, and you know from personal, emotional experience, that human beings are wired for connection. People crave relationships and to feel connected to other people. Your relationships and connections with those other weird creatures who are humans just like you are tender spots for us.

Relationships are often named by my clients as the most vulnerable aspect of their lives. For me, relationships, and especially intimate relationships are one of the most tender spots on my heart and my soul. When we feel deep trust and belonging with our very best friends, when we feel the incomparable experience of being in love or the unwavering camaraderie of being a part of a team, we feel most alive. It makes sense, then, that when those relationships aren't going as we'd like, it feels a bit like we're dying. Feeling disconnected from others can be devastating simply because it's the opposite of connection. And connection makes us feel most alive.

Naturally, your eating disorder recognizes that relationships are powerful and, therefore, can be used as highly effective weapons. Recall how we examined how all-or-none thinking drops a bomb on your self-esteem. Now imagine your eating disorder deploying a missile toward the key foundational pillars in your life: trust, hope, faith, support, and connection. The eating disorder absolutely weaponizes one of our most profound gifts of human connection and sabotages our relationships with others.

Relationships have been demonstrated in research as being sources of meaning, a protective factor against the effects of anxiety, depression, and even suicide. Of course, your eating disorder isn't going to allow you to have strong social support because this would get in the way of the eating disorder's mission to keep itself going.

Think of your most recent interactions with others. I'm guessing many of the times you spent time with friends or with family, there was food involved—or there could have been food involved if your eating disorder didn't stop you from grabbing dinner with your loved ones. The eating disorder will apply all-or-none thinking to eating, particularly in front of other people.

For example, your eating disorder may have determined that gluten is, in fact, the devil. Your best friend invites you out for a coffee date to catch up since you haven't seen her in a while. She suggests the local coffee shop with its most amazing latte that you two used to get together, admiring how the baristas make art out of the steamed milk on top. You agree to the coffee date though you've promised your eating disorder you won't disobey its rigid rules, because if you do you'll have FAILED; you'll only get a drip coffee. No cream. Cream isn't okay either, even though its's gluten-free.

You arrive at the charming coffee shop and fondly remember all the times you've met your friend for coffee. You walk to the counter to order, only to be faced with the pastry case next to the register. Shit. It's loaded with delicious pastries, looking almost like something out of a fairytale. You look over your options: beautiful croissants, lovely scones, sumptuous muffins, but nothing gluten-free. Shit!

Here, all-or-none thinking widens its grasp from the rigid food rules and opens up to include your thoughts about your friend. "What the hell was she thinking, inviting me here?! I mean, I know we used to come here together but she also knows I don't eat gluten anymore. Because gluten is terrible. You know what? She's terrible! She clearly doesn't care at all about me. We're so different, we probably shouldn't even be friends anymore." And just like that, your eating disorder threw a grenade into that relationship and booby-trapped that coffee date.

Several things occurred in this example. First, we know that the inflexible food rules apply all-or-none thinking. Second, the all-or-none thinking from the food rules "othered" you. *Othering* is a phenomenon in which people feel different from the mainstream. When you are *othered*, you feel different in a bad way. Here, your eating disorder's rule of no gluten made you feel different, like you couldn't participate, like you didn't deserve the pastry, like you weren't allowed it.

The third way all-or-none thinking happened in the example was in the conclusions your eating disorder drew about your friend. According to your eating disorder, she obviously doesn't care about you at all; your entire friendship up to this point could be completely tossed aside. The idiom, "throwing the baby out with the bathwater" is all-or-none thinking and that's what your eating disorder did with your trip to the coffee shop.

Let's tie this back to what was initially discussed in this section. Relationships and human connections make you feel most alive. Moreover, they are protective factors against numerous difficulties and illnesses and rank among your most significant assets in recovery. All-or-none thinking makes it possible for you to take the gift of your relationship with your friend, the opportunity to connect with her over coffee at a shop that is meaningful to you, and to twist that into a reason to disconnect, judge her, isolate, and withdraw into a world of rigid food rules.

The eating disorder didn't just distance you from your friend. It completely disconnected you from her. Your eating disorder will cause you to draw dangerous, rash, unfounded conclusions that will damage your relationships with others, and this jeopardizes your recovery because it robs you of support, meaning, and connection.

Treatment

EATING disorders love to apply all-or-nothing thinking to treatment. Making the choice to enter treatment—especially higher levels of care such as residential, partial-hospitalization, and intensive outpatient programming—is brave and badass. There's no way around it.

Treatment is an investment, one of the biggest anyone can make. Investing requires that you take a risk and that you sacrifice. With treatment, you take risks by not knowing exactly what the outcome will be, how long treatment will take, how much pain you'll go through in the process. The risks are also in not knowing what tasks you'll need to complete, what feelings you will need to face, which foods you'll need to eat, or weight you may need to gain. The mere act of willingly (or at least somewhat willingly) walking into the unknown with hope for a better future is a big, big risk. Big risks necessitate big, brave souls to meet the challenge. Guess what? That's what you've got!

Investment also requires sacrifice. Sacrifice is giving up something or going through something difficult to get a greater reward in return. It is rare those returns on investment are immediate. In treatment, you make many sacrifices; many people have to put their lives on hold to make time to go to treatment. Treatment costs money, too, often significant amounts. Treatment may mean you have to gain weight which might be your greatest fear, although really, this is your eating disorder's greatest fear, not yours. Treatment means you have to sacrifice comfort and familiarity for learning, to do therapy, and to feel the most painful feelings you have now and have likely been avoiding for a very long time. Sacrifice hurts.

The sacrifices and risks from your investment in treatment, and your recovery overall, will yield dividends unlike anything else you've experienced. Recovery is *always* worth it.

Treatment means investing in your health, your understanding of yourself, your emotional wellbeing, and your future. Now, let's consider treatment from your eating disorder's perspective. The goal of treatment is to help you get rid of the eating disorder. As you may have guessed, your eating disorder isn't going to like this. And, treatment is hard; it requires that you directly face food, stop using eating disorder behaviors, and feel your feelings.

To your eating disorder, this sounds awful. Your eating disorder will do anything to trick you into believing treatment isn't worth it, that you can't live through the sacrifice, and that the risks are far too scary to take. All lies. To deter you from treatment, your eating disorder will apply all-or-none thinking.

All-or-none thinking shows up with treatment in several ways. First, your eating disorder might use all-or-none thinking as you decide that you need to enter treatment. For example, you decide to call an eating disorder treatment center you are interested in and you speak with a nice intake clinician you connect with; she answers all your questions and you decide you'd like to start attending. She explains they don't have a spot open for you to start this week but you can start next week instead. Immediately, all-or-none thinking comes in. and tells you "Oh, see; this just isn't going to work out for you at all."

And just like that, all the courage you mustered up and the time spent gathering information, and all the connection formed with the intake clinician are washed down the drain. Either you can get in this week or screw it all because it's probably not going to work anyway! Things need to go perfectly or you're completely unwilling to engage with them.

Other examples may look something like finding out you'll have a roommate in treatment, or realizing you'll have to eat your scariest fear food, or being told you'll have to do group therapy with strangers. You decide that one factor is worth completely giving up on treatment; it's either going to be exactly as you want it or you're not doing it at all.

Another common way your eating disorder manipulates you with all-or-none thinking is by making you afraid of how you're going to do in treatment as if it's a performance. If you have an eating disorder, you're most likely very high-achieving, hard-working, conscientious, and think the idea of letting other people down or being found out as less than perfect is the worst thing possible. Naturally, your eating disorder will utilize this to intimidate you and distort the facts.

Treatment is not about performance. No one gets an A+ by recovering perfectly. There are no awards for being the fastest to recover, the best at recovery, or the most liked person in treatment. But, your eating disorder will plant these fears in you. "What if I take forever to get better?" "What will my family think if I can't gain weight?" "What if my therapist doesn't like me?" "What will I do when the others in treatment do better than I do?"

The eating disorder will make you so afraid of these things that it will offer up the idea that perhaps you shouldn't even bother with treatment in the first place. You should quit. Or, if you do stick in there with treatment, all the good work you've done somehow doesn't count because you can call to mind times when you've "failed." Remember, with all-or-none thinking, perfection at all times is your only option.

Perfection is not applicable to treatment or recovery. Do yourself a favor and get that out of your head. That's out of bounds because it's not possible, and treatment isn't about performance either. All-or-none thinking is the warped way your eating disorder makes treatment all about perfection and performance, so it can sabotage you, hoping that you will completely give up or throw away all of your hard work.

The Takeaway

ALL-OR-NONE THINKING sets you up for failure by using an impossible standard. No one can be perfect or perform perfectly at all times. All-or-none thinking is a setup because it does not allow for struggle, failure, or any shades of gray which are necessary and unavoidable in recovery. All-or-none thinking causes you to lose sight of what's important and will encourage you to impulsively toss aside truth and reason. See all-or-nothing thinking for what it is: a trick, a trap your eating disorder uses to make you give up on recovery and feel awful about yourself.

8

OVERGENERALIZATION

Overgeneralization is a common cognitive distortion wherein we draw a broad, sweeping conclusion based on one piece or several small pieces of data. Overgeneralization usually involves you calling to mind one incident where you didn't measure up and using that to make conclusions about the future, often that the future will continue to be filled with hardship and failure.

With overgeneralization, there just aren't enough data points to draw a realistic, truthful conclusion. Commonly, overgeneralization functions to strengthen negative beliefs about ourselves.

Let's say you've been having a difficult year filled with tough times in work or school and with struggles in your friendships and/or romantic relationships all on top of the hardship of living with an eating disorder. In this situation, it's understandable you might feel as though things will continue to feel difficult and not go your way.

However, feelings are feelings, not facts. Though you may *feel* as if things will continue to go poorly, that might not be true in reality. It's dangerous to draw conclusions about your recovery based on current upset emotions, even if there are valid reasons to feel upset. Again, it makes sense why you might feel like things will continue to feel like a struggle in the future, but you can empower yourself by remembering that *feelings are feelings*, not facts.

Eating disorders love to exploit your fears using overgeneralization. Overgeneralization is a powerful cognitive distortion used by eating disorders because overgeneralization means you're drawing faulty conclusions, usually about the future and about yourself. With overgeneralization, the conclusions arrived at are big, bad, and sweeping.

Eating disorders love to help you call to mind the one time you failed, the time you ate something that wasn't helpful to your recovery, the one time you were socially awkward or late for work, or the one person who doesn't like you. In all these examples, there's only one piece—or maybe a few pieces—of data. That's all it takes for your eating disorder to draw a faulty conclusion using overgeneralization.

For example, you've been dealing with your eating disorder for several years. Recently, you've decided you want to pursue recovery with all you've got; a high-five to you! You've been in therapy for a couple of months and you're continuing to have episodes of binges most days of the week. Your eating disorder tells you its verdict. "You're still bingeing, even after committing to recovery and even after therapy. You're never going to recover."

Bingo.

That's one of the most common eating disorder lies brought to you courtesy of overgeneralization. *You're never going to recover.* Can you hear the fear in that? I can. That's why it's so powerful. The eating disorder is planting fear in you so you'll give up on recovery and let the eating disorder stay in your life.

Fear can be intimidating. But, let's set that to the side and take a gentle, but realistic, look at that same example. You've been struggling with binge eating for years. You're new to recovery. You recently started therapy. Now, compare how much time in this example you've concentrated on recovery to how much time you were wrestling with the eating disorder on your own. No wonder you still have more days than not with binges; you're still practicing and this is a new way of living for you. Changing behavior takes time. Recovery takes time. Overgeneralizing in this example isn't realistic.

It's not fair to make a big, sweeping conclusions about the fate of your recovery based on your first two months in therapy. You don't have enough data to know what will happen. And, just so you know, your eating disorder is never going to be okay with you concluding you're capable of recovery.

Eating disorders love to use overgeneralization to make you feel afraid, hopeless and discouraged with your progress. Part of what makes overgeneralization so powerful, aside from the fear-mongering, is that the stakes are high with the conclusions you draw. Can I recover? Am I a good person? Is my life going to turn out okay? All of those are high stakes questions where the implications are big.

Overgeneralization draws inaccurate conclusions about these high stakes issues using faulty, little or no data at all. The following sections will explore how your eating disorder uses overgeneralization to draw false conclusions about food, yourself, others, and treatment.

Food

YOUR EATING DISORDER employs overgeneralization to distort your views on food. Earlier in this book, you learned how your eating disorder's mission is to keep itself going. Overgeneralization is a great way for your eating disorder to interfere with you having a healthy relationship with food. The previous example about trying to stop binge eating serves as a perfect illustration of overgeneralization with food; this overgeneralization tells you you'll never have a healthy, non-bingeing relationship with food.

Overgeneralization can appear in other ways as well. Your eating disorder may use overgeneralization to fool you into thinking you won't recover because you've been having difficulty with your meal plan. Let's say your dietitian creates a meal plan, you miss one of the food groups you're aiming for, and overgeneralization sweeps in, accusing you of always messing up your meal plan. Obviously, you'll never recover. Here, you see overgeneralization in its classic state. It's taking one instance—a limited piece of data—and creating a big, whopping conclusion that you are incapable of recovery.

Your eating disorder may also use overgeneralization when you are working to recover your relationship with fear foods or trigger foods. For example, some people who have foods they've binged on choose to temporarily stop eating those foods. During their break from these foods, they work with their treatment team to develop skills to use when they start eating the triggering foods again and work to repair their relationship with them.

Perhaps you've had a difficult time with your relationship with ice cream. Your eating disorder turned ice cream into your go-to binge food. After working with your treatment team, you decide you need to keep ice cream out of your freezer while you build skills in therapy and nutrition counseling. Time goes by, you've gained insight into why ice cream became the designated binge food, and you've added new tools to your toolbox to help you eat ice cream in proportion with your hunger and nutritional needs. After consulting with your treatment team, you decide it's time to re-introduce it into your diet and create a new, healthy relationship with ice cream.

It's your first week having ice cream back in stock in your freezer at home. One night, you begin eating ice cream, lose control, and wind up bingeing. You've got a choice about what conclusions you're going to draw about this experience. Enter, eating disorder overgeneralization. Your eating disorder will tell you, using overgeneralization, "See, you just can't handle ice cream. Ice cream will always be your binge food."

Overgeneralization is making a huge conclusion that you'll never be able to eat this food without bingeing based on the first time you reintroduced it into your diet. See how absurd that is? A more reasonable, and frankly, more realistic conclusion would be that you binged because it was the first week you'd had ice cream back in the house. You're still practicing. Remind yourself that these sort of things, these slips in behavior or relapses (or whatever term you feel most comfortable using) are completely normal and part of the process. Plus, you shouldn't forget the other five nights of this first week back with the ice cream where you did not binge on it. Give yourself credit where it's due.

In the previous example, you absolutely do not have enough data points, examples, or information to draw any conclusions about what your relationship with ice cream can be like. You have one example from a high pressure, first encounter following a break from the food. This is bad data because it's an outlier.

No other time you eat ice cream will be the first time after a break; therefore, much difficulty will be relieved simply by having repeated interactions (a.k.a. practice) eating ice cream. So, where's the danger in this conclusion? So what if you can't eat ice cream again? To many of you, I'm guessing the idea of never being able to eat ice cream again without bingeing is pretty depressing in itself.

Moreover, the negative emotions of hopelessness, discouragement, and fear brought about by overgeneralization set you up to use behaviors. If you think, "I'll never be able to eat ice cream without bingeing," then you won't! It gives you reason to give up on eating it without bingeing. The eating disorder will tell you, "What the heck, you can't eat ice cream normally. You might as well binge on it anyway." See the vicious cycle in action here?

You can draw more reasonable, helpful, and compassionate conclusions when you remove overgeneralization from the equation. Don't draw big conclusions without enough data points and seek the support and perspective of your treatment team. Eating disorder treatment professionals can offer you perspective and normalize concerns, reminding you that relapses are completely normal and that relapse is not the end of the world or of your recovery.

Self

YOUR EATING DISORDER will use overgeneralization to sabotage your recovery by causing you to draw faulty, high stakes conclusions about yourself. When you draw these faulty conclusions, you will have negative feelings toward yourself and then continue to use eating disorder behaviors.

Overgeneralizations related to self are particularly dangerous because they have big implications for who you are. How people think about themselves is critical, especially during a time as precarious as recovery. When you think of yourself in a negative light, as undeserving, less than adequate, or not good enough, you're likely to act in accordance with those beliefs. Using eating disorder behaviors, which are physically and psychologically harmful to you, is a way of acting in line with negative beliefs about yourself.

Keep in mind the formula for overgeneralization: one part bad, little, or no data plus one part faulty conclusion with massive implications, in this case about yourself. An example I commonly see in people with eating disorders is that they frequently conclude that they're not good enough. Determining you're not good enough, or maybe even that you are bad, unworthy, or completely worthless, is a big damn deal. That conclusion is not going to help you recover; you're absolutely setting yourself up to use behaviors because they feel congruent with these negative beliefs. Using those behaviors repeatedly, in turn, deepens those beliefs like ruts in a road. The deeper the belief is, the truer it will feel.

Earlier in the book, you read how eating disorders hate imperfection, unexpected change, and failures even though all these processes are completely normal, *necessary* parts of life. Your eating disorder will take these normal occurrences and warp them using overgeneralization.

I can recall my eating disorder playing this trick with me, deepening the rut of my belief that I wasn't good enough. Actually, I had a deeply-held belief that not only was I not good enough but that things would never go my way. I was doomed to experience bad fortune my whole life. Admittedly, it's quite melodramatic.

If you look at your eating disorder beliefs, you'll see a familiar theme of melodramatic, extreme thoughts. During my eating disorder, anytime a failure, unexpected change, or imperfection happened, my eating disorder used overgeneralization to make me feel profoundly worthless.

I remember getting my first speeding ticket. Getting a speeding ticket is certainly not the end of the world but because of my eating disorder's use of overgeneralization, I felt as though I'd never be able to forgive myself. I was driving down a road and didn't notice that the speed limit decreased. A cop spotted me, pulled me over, and gave me a speeding ticket. I'll tell you both versions of the story: the eating disorder version and then the version grounded in reality.

The eating disorder version of the story says that because I was already a good-for-nothing nobody destined to only have bad things come her way, I got a speeding ticket. The speeding ticket was confirmation of these negative beliefs about myself. "Only a terrible person would screw up like that. I can't believe myself. Honestly, how dumb am I? Bad things like this always happen to me. It's just like that week when my computer broke." Using the formula for overgeneralization, you can see the eating disorder is taking this one example, one limited experience of getting a speeding ticket, and is forming a grand conclusion about me—that I'm no good and bad things always happen to me.

The second version of the story, the one that's, you know, based in reality, says I wasn't paying enough attention this one time, missed the speed limit sign, and got caught.

Getting speeding tickets is common. Do I want to drive safely? You bet. Did I make a mistake by not doing so that time? Definitely. Is it fair to conclude I'm worthless and destined for misery because of this? Of course not, but that's what happened. You'd better believe that I felt so guilty and miserable about myself that I believed I'd keep getting knocked down by little scuffles. And of course, I wound up using behaviors big time. The eating disorder can't allow you to see things realistically or flexibly and to understand we all make mistakes.

I've spent many sessions with clients helping them sift through the ways their eating disorder is exploiting them using overgeneralization. One of my clients will get fired from a job, have someone break up with them, or have one of their kids say, "I hate you" out of anger. Their eating disorder takes these few limited examples, bad data points, and uses those to come to conclusions such as, "I'm no good in my career. I shouldn't even try," "I'm terrible in relationships. Everyone always leaves me," and "I'm an awful parent. My kids hate everything I do."

You don't have enough evidence from any of the previous scenarios to make a grand conclusion such as being a bad parent. You only have one example. Even when you have a few examples such as being broken up with, you have to check that against how common an occurrence it is for people in general. Breakups are normal. Being fired isn't unheard of. And, kids say hurtful things out of anger to their parents.

If you can see difficult experiences for what they are— simply difficult experiences you can learn from—instead of seeing them as evidence that you and your future are crap, you will be able to resist using eating disorder behaviors much more easily. Understanding overgeneralization can help you recover your perspective about yourself and your future.

Others

ANOTHER DAMAGING WAY eating disorders use overgeneralization is with your conclusions about other people. We've talked about how relationships with others and human connection is essential to health and happiness. Naturally, your eating disorder is going to sabotage your relationships given that they are so important.

Here's how it works. Eating disorders have no perspective on anything, including the nature of relationships. Relationships alone are difficult enough for most people to make sense of without an eating disorder on their back. Having relationships with other people means some things are inevitable: heartache, misunderstanding, disappointment, to name a few. The rewards of relationships greatly outweigh the difficult aspects but not in the eyes of your eating disorder.

Your eating disorder will take the normal costs of being in relationships with others (heartache, misunderstanding, and disappointment) and will draw unfounded, rash, damaging conclusions. Let's explore this more.

One of my clients recently shared that she'd only been on a few dates with a person she liked. One night after their date, she was waiting for his reply to her text message. He didn't text back that night. There are many reasons that could explain why this person didn't reply to the text right away. He could have been busy. He could have fallen asleep. He could have been trying to play it cool after the date and didn't want to come across too strong. His phone could have died or fallen in the toilet. Perhaps he read the text and was interrupted before he could reply.

All these are normal explanations that aren't cause for concern. And, he usually did respond to her texts. My client's eating disorder, however, took that normal situation and a single example of data and blew it up into a self-esteem assault. Her eating disorder told her, "He's not texting me back. He's not going to text me back. I'm so worried he didn't like me because I wasn't thin enough. I bet it actually *was* because I'm not thin enough. Dating is awful. My body is awful." And then, she binged followed by a whole day of restricting all food the next day.

Her eating disorder hooked her with the extreme, high-stakes and negative global conclusions it came to. After talking with my client in session about this, she was able to have more compassion for herself knowing her eating disorder was effective at using overgeneralization. She was able to gently remind herself of all the reasons that could account for him not replying to her text that night, that had absolutely nothing to do with her weight. Just as an aside, he replied the following morning!

The brilliance of the eating disorder's use of overgeneralization shows in the results it got. The eating disorder got her to use behaviors; that's its mission—to keep itself going. Overgeneralization is also brilliant because relationships are always going to provide you with small or bad examples fit for distortion.

We can all call to mind a time when we let someone down when we forgot to return a call, we were late getting an assignment in to our teammates at work, forgot an important anniversary or celebration, we said something that we intended to sound one way but came out wrongly. I bet we've all said something hurtful simply because we were overwhelmed with anger and were caught up in the passion of the moment. Does that mean we're bad people only capable of treating others badly? Absolutely not. But, wouldn't it be great for your eating disorder's agenda if you bought into that?

Treatment

IF YOU BUY into the lies created by overgeneralization, treatment is going to sound like an extremely unappealing option and when you're in treatment, your eating disorder is going to try to kill your hopes of recovery. Relapse and struggle are necessary, unavoidable parts of treatment and recovery. Imagine how your eating disorder will use this against you, to halt your progress and lead you to the conclusion you can't recover.

That's usually the conclusion your disorder comes to about treatment. You can't do treatment. You'll never recover. And, if your eating disorder's going for the jugular, your whole life is going to consist of nothing but misery and suffering. The underlying message is the same: Give up now, continue to use behaviors, continue in your eating disorder. This should sound familiar by this point. It continues to come to the same terrible, predictably boring conclusion.

Keeping that conclusion in mind, let's review some examples of moments in recovery (via limited or bad pieces of data) that your eating disorder will twist to fool you. One that comes to mind for me was when one of my clients, after months and months of trying to decide whether she needed to go to inpatient treatment, bravely decided that she did, in fact, need to seek a higher level of care. I can't state emphatically enough how courageous that decision is and how gutsy it is to pursue treatment despite feeling terrified about what the treatment will be like. She chose a treatment center, screwed up her courage, and dialed the phone number for the intake line.

It went to voicemail.

My client was devastated. The mere act of making that call felt, to her, like it took all the strength she could muster. She could have thought to herself, "Wow, that was so disappointing! I feel so deflated after that call went to voicemail. I was really hoping someone would have picked up. I feel like the wind was let out of my sails. But, I left a message and I'll look forward to when they call me back."

That is a compassionate, realistic thought based on a small piece of data in the phone not being answered. This is how her eating disorder interpreted the event using overgeneralization: "See, this isn't going to work out. What kind of a place is this anyway? It's like they don't care about their patients at all. Maybe they have too many patients if they're too busy to pick up the phone. Maybe I won't go to a higher level of care. I don't think it's for me. They probably won't call back anyway." This harmful conclusion was drawn based on the same precipitating event, the phone going to voicemail. The difference was in the distortion from overgeneralization.

Overgeneralization is commonly used by eating disorders to deter you from seeking treatment and sticking it out when treatment gets tough, as treatment always does. Of course, your eating disorder does this; it wants to keep the status quo. It wants you to stay and spend all your time with it. It definitely doesn't want you to move on. Treatment is the ultimate step toward moving on and your eating disorder simply can't accept that. Knowing that your eating disorder is not going to be okay with you seeking treatment, you can be on the lookout for overgeneralization.

The Takeaway

OVERGENERALIZATION IS dangerous because the conclusions you draw about your recovery and yourself are negative and significant. The good news, though, is that overgeneralization has an easily recognizable pattern, always involving a small, inaccurate, or bad piece of data, example, or life experience. That small example is then linked to monumental, unreasonable, negative conclusions, usually about your future and yourself.

When you notice your eating disorder using overgeneralization to make you feel afraid or give up, take a step back and add some self-compassion. Do some perspective-taking and question whether the conclusion is reasonable, realistic, or helpful. Ask yourself if you need more data than one example of hardship, and commit to gathering more examples before coming to a grand conclusion.

9

DISCOUNTING THE POSITIVE

If you have an eating disorder, you discount the positive—or rather, your eating disorder discounts it. Discounting the positive is as it sounds. Discounting the positive is when you minimize or dismiss positive experiences, convincing yourself that those positives don't matter. Discounting the positive happens when you brush aside legitimate signs of strength or progress.

It's important to accurately evaluate what's going well or what you're *doing* well and what's not going as well as you'd like. In recovery, you'll have both areas of strength and areas for improvement. When your eating disorder discounts the positive, it causes you to ignore a huge chunk of crucial data. When it discounts the positive, it's impossible for you to see the full picture and if you don't have an accurate picture of where you're at in recovery, you won't be able to progress.

Discounting the positive in eating disorder recovery is like navigating in your car to a new destination. Have you ever had that experience when your GPS or navigation app is guiding you along the route but isn't showing the correct location? You've actually passed that step in the directions but the navigation system hasn't caught up with how far you've come. You're one mile farther down the road than it's showing? It's problematic! You can't move ahead to where you need to be until it recognizes your progress. The same principle extends to recovery. You're not going to get further into recovery until you give yourself credit for progress you've already made.

Your eating disorder will do anything to prevent you from recognizing your progress. Sometimes, discounting the positive is obvious. You clearly kick butt at something or have a wonderful strength to offer the world, but your eating disorder invalidates that 100%, telling you your progress or gift doesn't matter at all. Other times, your eating disorder discounts the positive in a more subtle, insidious way. For example, you worked hard over the week on reducing your eating disorder behaviors; you went a whole six days without purging, a huge accomplishment for you! You've never had that long a streak without purging, but your eating disorder can't allow you to recognize, let alone celebrate, this awesome stretch of progress.

When you show up to your therapy appointment, you immediately begin to tell your therapist about the one time during the whole week that you did purge. Your eating disorder convinced you the six days without purging didn't matter as much as the one day you purged. As a treatment professional, I can tell you this is a common occurrence; my clients consistently report on their weaknesses, completely discounting all the good things they've done.

At this point, you might be wondering what the big deal is with discounting the positive? Okay, you know it might not be the best approach but perhaps it doesn't seem like it's the most harmful thing your eating disorder uses against you? Wrong. Discounting the positive is extremely damaging to your recovery, not to mention to your self-esteem.

To go back to the example of the client who reports on the one time he or she purged rather than the six days they went behavior-free, imagine how different each of those therapy sessions could be. In one of those sessions, the client focuses on the one weakness (or area for growth, or struggle point—however you see it) and likely spends the session re-hashing the week's negatives. This is an important part of therapy. It's important to honestly—but gently—look at what needs improvement and work, but it's equally important to examine what you're doing right, what's going well, and what you're bringing to the game.

If that same client had begun by sharing that they went six whole days without purging, the tone of the session would be different. They'd get to celebrate with the therapist and spend time in session breaking down the factors that helped them have such a great week in recovery. The same applies to you; if you're unwilling or unable to look at what you've done well, you're not likely to identify those strategies or use them in the future. This is critical. Can you see how this would please your eating disorder? Discounting the positive keeps you stuck in a negative rut even when it's not the truth. The truth in this example is that the client had a strong week in recovery and deserves to celebrate his or her progress.

The eating disorder tricks you into thinking you're less recovered than you actually are when it discounts the positive. Your eating disorder will do anything to keep itself going, to stay on target with its mission. Imagine if you gave yourself credit for how much recovery you have under your belt! You might feel empowered, hopeful, proud of yourself. Those feelings would be incredible and inspiring.

Those feelings, however, are not congruent with using eating disorder behaviors. If you're feeling empowered, hopeful, and proud of yourself, how likely are you to have an all-out binge/purge/restrict/over-exercise bender? Not nearly as likely as you would be if you discounted the positive and wound up feeling powerless, hopeless, and thoroughly ashamed of yourself. Your eating disorder needs you to feel those incredibly negative, painful emotions because it keeps you using eating disorder behaviors.

Discounting the positive is used by your eating disorder within all four categories discussed in this book: food, self, others, and treatment. The following sections examine in depth how your eating disorder discounts the positive to keep you stuck in your disorder.

Food

FOR MOST PEOPLE IN RECOVERY, food becomes ground zero for battling with your eating disorder. Eating disorders have rigid rules about food. Earlier in the book, you explored how dichotomous, all-or-none thinking is applied to food and how overgeneralization creates big, unhelpful conclusions from little or no data. Discounting the positive fits in similarly with how your eating disorder distorts your perspective about food. This can happen in several ways.

One way is by eating disorders twisting your views about a specific food. Your eating disorder is so rigid that it won't recognize the good in those foods. It's either categorized as a good food or a bad food. For instance, pizza. I haven't yet met a client with an eating disorder whose eating disorder thought pizza was acceptable to eat. However, barring any major medical conditions diagnosed by a licensed medical professional, people can include pizza in their diet while maintaining their health.

Your eating disorder will try to trick you into thinking everything about pizza is bad, maybe even evil, and screws up your health. This is discounting all the positives of pizza. First, pizza is delicious and deliciousness should count! Pizza can also get you necessary carbohydrates for the day as well as some protein and fats from cheese. Pizza can even get you some veggie servings depending on the toppings you choose. Again, excluding medical conditions wherein pizza truly isn't a good option, it can be incorporated into your diet without concern.

Your eating disorder discounts the positive by convincing you there are no nutrients in pizza at all. A more realistic perspective would be to step back and ask, "What nutrients have I gotten today? Would pizza provide me with some of the nutrients I'm still trying to get in today? Yes, actually, I think pizza would be a fine choice today. And I can trust my body to handle pizza."

Discounting the positive occurs not only with specific foods—by not seeing them realistically and instead completely demonizing them—but also happens on a broader level with whole food groups. One case in point would be carbohydrates. Carbohydrates are a macronutrient essential for your survival; they provide you with energy for your daily life and critical functions such as breathing, thinking, keeping your heart beating in addition to other activities such as walking, biking, running, or even playing pick-up basketball. Carbohydrates are fuel, and fuel is necessary for living. When I say necessary, I mean *you can't skip it*, not without major physical and mental health consequences.

I remember working with a client who was struggling

with restricting and purging. In session, we examined the food rules her eating disorder imposed upon her. She shared, "I don't eat carbs. Carbs are bad. There's nothing redeeming about them. Carbs only make you fat." I've certainly heard similar things in different forms throughout my years of practice. I asked, "Tell me what you know about the benefits of carbohydrates. I mean, if they're so bad why do people have to eat them as part of a balanced diet?" She replied quickly and emphatically, *"There are no good things about carbs. Carbs are the enemy."* At that moment, I knew I was speaking with her eating disorder, not her. I was actively engaging with the eating disorder, challenging its logic, and her eating disorder hated that.

After further exploration, she explained that because she didn't believe there was anything good to be gained from eating any carbohydrates at all, she did that. She simply didn't eat any carbohydrates... except when she binged on all-carbohydrate foods: chips, cookies, tortillas, popcorn. The client also talked at length about being an athlete and how she often felt sluggish or fatigued. She shared how sometimes it was difficult to complete her exercise routine.

Her eating disorder discounted all the positives about carbohydrates, placing them completely off limits for her to eat which, in turn, resulted in her having carbohydrate binge-and-purge episodes. Her eating disorder took away all the positives so she'd remove carbs from her diet and be set up to use behaviors later, specifically to binge on carbs. Her eating disorder discounted completely all the positives of an entire food group, to keep her stuck.

Another way eating disorders discount the positive is shown in the example at the beginning of this chapter where the client who went six days without bingeing couldn't give themselves credit for that wonderful victory. With food, no one does things "perfectly." What would that even mean, to eat perfectly?

Eating perfectly might be defined in unhealthy, skewed ways by your eating disorder, e.g. *eat tons of veggies, don't eat carbs, snacks can only be proteins.* Blah, blah, blah. That doesn't sound perfect and certainly doesn't sound healthy. When your eating disorder discounts the positive, it distorts reality and leads you into behaviors because, according to your eating disorder, you've nothing to be proud of anyway.

Self

PEOPLE WITH EATING disorders regularly fall prey to discounting the positive, especially about themselves. Discounting the positive leads you to downplay your strengths and causes you to make decisions out of fear or feelings of inadequacy. It prevents you from recognizing your growth. When you succumb to your positives being eroded away, you fall far and hard, sinking deeper into negative beliefs about yourself and only making recovery more difficult.

Discounting the positive, particularly in terms of your view of yourself, is about diminishing your progress and downplaying your power. Your eating disorder does not want you to notice or celebrate your progress. Your eating disorder also doesn't want for you to connect with your innate power. Human beings are extraordinary; I'm sure you can conjure up stories of people overcoming adversity, doing big things that change the world for the better, or simply knocking things out into the stratosphere in an area important to them.

I bet you've had a time in your life where you completely kicked ass too. Perhaps you've even had a time in your life where you worked slowly, gradually, and diligently, chipping away at a goal that is truly important to you. You had to be in touch with your positives, your progress, and your strengths, to accomplish those things. Do you remember when you finally made it to the end of a long goal or when someone told you that what you did mattered to them? It felt wonderful and fulfilling. It feels exciting and deeply satisfying when you're connected to your positives, when you can breathe them in and—if able to truly embrace them —when you allow yourself to revel.

If it feels so good, deep-down-in-your-soul good, then why discount the positive? Aside from embracing your strengths being completely out of line with your eating disorder's agenda, people I've talked with share other reasons for holding back and minimizing their awesomeness.

One common source I've run into is messages received from family or friend groups. One client I had explained she couldn't complete a journal assignment I'd given her for the week because discounting the positives had become a deeply entrenched pattern for her. I asked her to write in her journal each day, making a list of all the things she did that were recovery-oriented behaviors, such as being kind to herself. This client bristled when I explained the assignment to her, sharing, "But that makes me feel like I'd be bragging, and bragging is rude."

We talked further and she shared that she grew up in a home where she wasn't supposed to "get too big for her britches" or draw attention to herself. It must have been difficult for her given that she's such a smart, hard-working, kind, helpful person. Many people with eating disorders fit that description. I can personally relate to this, having been raised with the idea you shouldn't "toot your own horn."

In school, even when I would win awards or perform, I'd respond to any compliments with some form of the classic discounting/minimizing such as, "Well, I'm happy about it too but I'm lucky because there weren't very many people competing," or, "My solo was good but so-and-so's was better," or, the ever popular, "I've still got a lot to learn." Yes, of course, everyone still has a lot to learn; this doesn't diminish the goodness of what they did or who they are.

I've noticed women are especially prone to discounting the positive even when the positive isn't directly related to eating disorder recovery. Culturally, women who are in touch with their inner strengths are shamed back into a power-down position. They're called arrogant, or masculine or intimidating.

Women who not only feel connected to their inner strengths but who can speak intelligently about them, and who can take ownership of their assets get called bitches. It's not fair. And, unfortunately, it happens.

No one wants to be thought of as arrogant, big-headed or out of touch with reality, one who overestimates their ability. We have become so caught up in the fear of being perceived that way, that we cower, afraid to step on anyone's toes. Nobody wants to offend anyone else; worse, we're afraid if we own our strengths, particularly in front of others, in public, those people will disagree with our assessment of ourselves. People feel afraid others won't see their greatness, and they're afraid of making a fool of themselves.

Your eating disorder *loves* that this fear is culturally supported, especially for women. The cultural support for this fear allows your eating disorder to make the fear seem more real, more dangerous. Though their experience is different, men are hurt by shrinking from their strengths as well.

When you shrink, discount your strengths and hide your light, other people and your eating disorder are free to push you around, keep you in a power-down position, and saddest of all, stuck in a state of doubting your worth or feeling worthless outright.

It's near impossible to recover when you're in the power-down position. Doubting your worth, strengths, and abilities is the ideal position for you to continue using eating disorder behaviors, thinking vicious, self-defeating thoughts, and remaining stuck in your eating disorder.

The fear of overestimating your strengths and, even scarier, having other people out you about it, feels incredibly intense and powerful. It seems like the consequences of thinking highly of yourself could be painful. You might even encounter shame. Your eating disorder wants you to forget that the consequences of hiding your strengths are much worse. Author Marianne Williamson wrote in her book, *A Return to Love*, the following:

> *Our deepest fear is not that we are inadequate. It is that we are powerful beyond measure. It is our light, not our darkness that frightens us... Your playing small does not serve the world. There is nothing enlightened about shrinking so that other people won't feel insecure around you.*

Your eating disorder forces you to play small. Your eating disorder forces you to stay scared. Your eating disorder is frightened, terrified even, of your light. If you truly want to recover, you're going to have to step into the light instead of hiding it. You need to stop discounting your positives, and denying, hiding, and minimizing your strengths. Get out there and swing for the fences.

Others

MUCH LIKE YOUR eating disorder discounts the positives in you, it tempts and tricks you into discounting them in others. Discounting the positive in others makes you more vulnerable to using eating disorder behaviors and far less likely to recover. Sometimes when thinking of other people, it's easy for us to call to mind times when others were unkind, unreliable or downright mean.

Surely, there are valid reasons for feeling reluctant to interact with, get in relationships with, and rely on others. Other people can be hurtful or absent, or they can abandon you or be judgmental. We, ourselves, can be those things too. We have to gently remind ourselves when we think "other people suck" that sometimes we *are* the other person who sucks. Nobody's exempt.

Just as you are not all negative, other people aren't either. For every example you can cite of other people letting you down, you can remember times when others were exactly what you needed. You can't ignore how much joy you've experienced in conversation with good friends, or discount how connecting deeply with another person makes you feel profoundly less alone in your struggles. Even with people who are difficult for you to interact with, it's difficult to deny how much they can teach you, especially about yourself.

Your eating disorder discounts the positive in others to reduce your likelihood of reaching out for support, yet support from others is an incredible recovery resource.

Everyone needs a cheerleader now and then, and having a friend commiserate with you and empathize when you're down is priceless. If you felt less alone in your struggles and had someone to cheer you on through a rough patch, your eating disorder would be weaker.

Your eating disorder will be critical of people who could potentially support you by trying to convince you they don't have enough to offer. If you reach out to your best friend who has never had an eating disorder, what good is that going to do? It would probably be incredibly helpful, which scares the hell out of your eating disorder.

Your eating disorder minimizes how amazing your friends, co-workers, teachers, partners, and family members have been. Pause for a moment and think of how it feels when your eating disorder discounts your own positives. Now, allow yourself to feel the impact of your eating disorder doing this very same thing to the people you love the most. It's unfair, inaccurate, and mean of your eating disorder to do so.

The way your eating disorder discounts the positive can have an even deeper, more negative impact. Let's take the idea of your eating disorder discounting the positive in other people and extend it out into the future. If your eating disorder fools you into believing other people don't have enough positive to offer you, you will treat them in accordance with this belief. You're set up to connect less, decline invitations to get together, and to become critical of other people's support; you're set up to believe they can't help you anyway.

For example, you are thinking of talking to your mother about how recovery has been lately. You think your mom is pretty darn great. Overall, she's supportive, interested in your life, and you know she loves you. You consider your mom one of the closest people to you. She is a safe person.

Enter, your eating disorder. All the things mentioned about your mother somehow don't count. According to your eating disorder, she's supportive but not supportive enough. She's interested but not interested enough; she's probably more interested in your sibling. She loves you but... really, does she love you in the right way?

Your eating disorder is going to trick you into thinking your mom's loving you isn't enough. If you take a breath and a moment to let this sink in, you can feel the sadness of what your eating disorder is doing. Moreover, once your eating disorder has you tricked through discounting the positive of your mom's love and support for you, making it seem less important than it is, you are more likely to act in a manner congruent with that belief. You are more likely to withdraw or not reach out to her, to experience her support of you as lacking even though it's not, and to start minimizing the importance of her support for you. Worse, you're going to start minimizing everything good about her as a human, forgetting the many ways your mother shines and brings strength to you.

If this scenario doesn't fit for you, that's okay. Think of another person you could use as an example. Your eating disorder will discount the positive with *anyone* who could be helpful to your recovery. Swap out "mother" in the example for anyone else: friend, boyfriend, girlfriend, spouse, family member, coach, or teacher. The list goes on. Your eating disorder would love you to underestimate or downplay how helpful others can be.

Your eating disorder thrives best when you are alone, or worse, when you're alone and you've slipped into a victim-like mindset characterized by thoughts like, "I'm alone and no one can get this." It requires more bravery to see others for all that they offer. It requires a ton of bravery to allow those other people to help you.

Treatment

OUT OF THE four domains discussed in the book (Food, Self, Others, and Treatment), Treatment is arguably the easiest domain to see how the eating disorder discounts the positive. It's not lost on me how difficult a decision it is to seek treatment, even more if that means seeking a higher level of care. I also readily acknowledge how much commitment, bravery, and grit it takes to get through treatment. With all those things out in the open, given the credit, recognition, and validation they deserve, it's necessary to discuss how your eating disorder discounts the positives about treatment.

Treatment is one of your eating disorder's favorite things to minimize, discount, and convince you not to pursue. It's clear your eating disorder benefits from clouding your ability to see the good things about your treatment. At the forefront of these good aspects of treatment is that you could gain significant recovery in treatment.

For some people, recovery begins in treatment at higher level of care. It's the beginning of a whole new way of living. Naturally, your eating disorder is going to hate this, doing anything possible to keep you from pursuing that treatment. You're going to be a heck of a lot less likely to go to treatment if you can't see and connect with the benefits of going.

Recall that our definition for discounting the positive is minimizing or discounting positive experiences, somehow convincing yourself they don't count. Your eating disorder is going to try to convince you that all the important components of treatment—as well as treatment overall—don't count either. One example of how this happens is with individual therapy. Your eating disorder will trick you into thinking that individual therapy won't have an impact on your life, or if it does, that it won't have enough of an impact to matter.

I remember from my own recovery my eating disorder telling me, "Therapy is fine but it's not making that much of a difference." Admittedly, therapy is only one to maybe two or three hours of your week, and progress in therapy—especially for people trying to recover from an eating disorder—is slow. It's important to have realistic expectations for therapy outcomes but equally important to fully recognize all that it can offer you. You have the potential to learn from individual therapy an unbelievable amount about yourself and about how to recover. Don't let your eating disorder discount this.

Another aspect of treatment eating disorders like to pick on is group therapy. Group therapy is a unique experience that offers you both support from others who are in similar situations, and feedback or perspective. I've worked with clients who were skeptical about group therapy as part of treatment. I've heard eating disorder comments such as, "How could any of these other people possibly relate to me?" "The other group members won't be as smart as I am and won't understand me," and, "Other group members are going to be sicker than I am and are going to bring me down."

I could go on and on with examples of how eating disorders discount the positives of group therapy. The end result, though, is the same. The eating disorder will convince you group therapy won't offer you something good enough to be worth the effort. In reality, however, group therapy can be a powerful facet of treatment that can strengthen recovery.

Eating disorders often convince people that the other group members somehow aren't good enough, aren't going to be able to help, and ultimately, aren't going to be able to understand. This is untrue. Clients I've worked with in group therapy shared their amazement at how much they had in common with other members despite vast differences in ages, life experiences, and differing eating disorder diagnoses. Groups can be one of the most intimate, connecting experiences someone can have. Looking at the situation honestly, without distortion, the power of groups cannot be discounted.

Finally, your eating disorder will absolutely discount the positive regarding higher level of care routes such as partial hospitalization or residential care. Part of the power of higher level of care options at those levels, in particular, is that you have to take a break from your life or most of the activities of your life, and focus solely on your treatment. Undoubtedly, this entails sacrifice. Perhaps you have to put work, school, family or social responsibilities on hold. It's a tough cost but comes with a potentially huge payout.

Your eating disorder will discount how significant it is to take a break from life and focus on recovering. Imagine if you could go to treatment, get away from all the places where your eating disorder triggers you, and to get away from people you need a break from, and to have your only task be focusing on your health.

Treatment at a higher level of care is a gift. There are limited experiences analogous to what higher level of care is really like. You don't often get an opportunity to devote all your energy toward your goal, in this case, recovery. Treatment heals through your concentrated effort, distance from stressors in your life, and immersion in a recovery-oriented environment with highly trained experts to help you at every step.

Treatment is an opportunity like no other. Treatment is an opportunity to create a better future for yourself. Your eating disorder simply doesn't want you to recognize the full value of what treatment can offer.

The Takeaway

YOUR EATING DISORDER will discount the positives in multiple areas of your life including food, yourself, other people, and treatment. Discounting the positive works by minimizing and making strengths and accomplishments smaller or less significant in your mind than they are in reality.

Discounting the positive sets you up to stay stuck in the eating disorder cycle because it impairs your ability to accurately assess what assets you bring to your recovery, how other people can support you, how food supports your recovery and fuels your life, and the ways in which treatment can dramatically change your life for the better.

As with our GPS metaphor at the beginning of the chapter, discounting the positive prevents you from tracking your progress, seeing how far you've come, and therefore, from being able to move forward in your recovery.

10

NEGATIVE FILTERING

Negative filtering is when you look at a situation and only focus on the negative parts, not the situation as it is in reality. Negative filtering is similar to some of the other cognitive distortions already discussed, and it also keeps you stuck in your eating disorder. With negative filtering, your awareness is only of the negatives, not the neutral or positive aspects. Imagine how much power this gives your eating disorder if you only see the negative parts of every experience.

Negative filtering is the corollary to discounting the positive, and is its ally; these tend to go hand-in-hand as you might have guessed. With negative filtering, you're not only ignoring any positives, but you're focusing too much on the not-so-good parts. When you reflect back on a situation, your eating disorder will use negative filtering to zoom in so closely on the negative part of the scenario that you cannot see anything else.

Much like discounting the positive, your eating disorder's negative filtering gives you an inaccurate picture of where you are in your recovery journey. You can't correctly assess your progress and plan for future recovery when you're zoomed in on the one bad thing that happened.

Negative filtering is also a powerful tool for your eating disorder to use because negative filtering can contribute to negative feelings about yourself, other people, food, treatment, and your future. Negative feelings about those areas result in hopelessness and a greater likelihood of continuing to use eating disorder behaviors.

Food

YOUR EATING DISORDER will use negative filtering to warp your view of food. This can happen with twisting the reality of a food itself or about your eating patterns overall. Let's revisit the pizza example from the chapter about discounting the positive.

Discounting the positive and negative filtering go together frequently. In discounting the positive, you saw how your eating disorder refused to acknowledge anything good about pizza, yet it's delicious and it has proteins, fats, and carbs you need for the day. Negative filtering is the complementary cognitive distortion.

You could think of them as the yin and yang of unhelpful thinking. Negative filtering with the pizza example would be thinking only of the "negative" things about pizza—how it's calorically dense, about the fat content, about how there can be processed food products in it, as a few examples. I intentionally placed "negative" in quotes since often, your eating disorder will take something not actually negative and will make it seem worse than it is using negative filtering.

In this example, it's not negative to eat something calorically dense or high in fat content. Your eating disorder is looking at one example of when you eat pizza and is zooming in, hyper-focusing on only "negative" aspects of the food, keeping you stuck in food rules and fearful of foods you needn't fear. Thus, the negative filtering is helping the eating disorder in its mission to keep itself going.

Your eating disorder may also apply negative filtering to your assessment of your eating patterns overall. When you look back on your week in food, perhaps when you meet with your therapist or dietitian, take note of what you speak about and what things draw your attention. If the only thing you find to bring up is the most difficult, weakest, worst part of your week, consider that your eating disorder might be negatively filtering.

One of your assignments from your treatment team could have been to eat a balanced breakfast each day. Your dietitian recommended this to help keep your hunger and blood sugar levels more stable, decreasing the likelihood of a binge episode later in the day. Over the seven days of the week, you missed breakfast on two of those days.

The first day you missed was the morning after being assigned the task of repairing your relationship with breakfast, and you missed this because you didn't plan enough time to prepare breakfast for yourself. Of course, you didn't! This is new to you! And that's *okay*. No need to judge yourself.

This is new learning, and new learning requires adjustment and kindness while you make those changes. The other day you missed was the one after you stayed up late with friends, out on the town. You had a great time; you were out there, living your life. This is also okay.

To your eating disorder, though, neither of these two

mornings can be okay. Your eating disorder is unreasonable, inflexible, and rigid. As we've established in this book, however, your eating disorder has little to no grounding in reality. The reality of the situation described in the afore-mentioned example is that you had five great days of approaching breakfast in a whole new way during the very first week you gave change a shot.

Negative filtering is rehearsing, remembering, and speaking to only the negative parts of the week. You can see as well that negative filtering's partner, discounting the posi-tive, is present. In the example, you don't get any credit for the five days you met your goals (discounting the positive) and you focus on or amplify your attention on the two days that didn't go as hoped (negative filtering).

Negative filtering can be a powerful tool for your eating disorder to use to sabotage your recovery, especially with regard to food itself or your eating patterns as a whole. Negative filtering shines a spotlight on the not-so-good or less-than-desirable parts of your week in food. However, those parts aren't necessarily the ones you need to attend to.

If you have an eating disorder, more likely than not you are hard on yourself, prone to self-criticism and probably feel tired or even demoralized by the recovery process. In times like these, you don't need to zoom in on and enlarge your failures; it's not motivating, inspiring, or helpful. That's why your eating disorder loves doing it. Working toward a more realistic, accurate view of food and your eating habits is how you can get back on track with recovery.

Self

NEGATIVE FILTERING about the self is wildly common among people with eating disorders who tend to be incredibly hard on themselves, though they're usually also intensely conscientious, hard-working, thoughtful, and kind souls. Negative filtering is one form of being too hard on yourself.

As we've seen with food, negative filtering isn't a fair depiction of whatever subject is at hand, and this is particularly concerning when the subject at hand is you.

Negative filtering narrows the focus of your attention, allowing in only the negative pieces of info; no positive, no neutral. Everyone has things they don't like about themselves and surely everyone has examples of things they've done that they don't like either. The key is to not let those poor actions or less-than-ideal pieces of who you are be the only story you tell yourself.

Over the course of several years, I once worked with a client who repeatedly spoke negatively about herself, regardless of how the situation truly was. She recounted in therapy, week after week, all the mistakes she believed she made. She thought she wasn't socially skilled enough. She thought she said something that sounded awkward to another person. She thought she sounded anxious or said hurtful things accidentally. If you asked her flat out—as I did—what she thought of herself, she'd tell you she's well-intentioned but socially awkward, as well as inexperienced, perfectionistic, and, of course, in her mind, "fat."

Her eating disorder used negative filtering to draw attention to and amplify the things she thought were negative, that made her self-conscious. In reality, she is wonderfully considerate, artistic, thoughtful, kind, and devoted to whatever she does or whomever she spends her time with. Her eating disorder used negative filtering to direct her focus to the things she didn't feel confident about, leaving out a key piece of the equation—all of her strengths.

For this client in particular, negative filtering functioned to keep her trapped in the belief she was less than adequate, not good enough, or even bad. When she connected with these negative, distorted beliefs about herself, she used restricting to punish herself by depriving herself of pleasure and to cause herself the pain she, on some level, believed she deserved.

The eating disorder's use of negative filtering can play out with body image as well. When you think of your body, what comes to mind? For most individuals with eating disorders, the first thing that comes to mind about their bodies is the body part they hate the most. Or, sometimes that they hate their body overall.

When I say, "What do you think of your body?" clients often reply with, "I hate my thighs," "I wish my arms weren't so big," "I would do anything to get my tummy flat," or the very vague yet very destructive response, "My body is fat." Here, the eating disorder is zooming in on the part of your body you think of as the worst or bad in some way. Notice how the body part you feel least comfortable with or toward which you hold most animosity is the only thing that comes to mind.

Negative filtering allows you to only see the "bad" parts of you, not your body as a realistic whole and not the things you like about your body. It's worth noting that the things that you consider negative or bad, or the sweeping, nebulous fat, are likely labeled those because of your eating disorder.

Without your eating disorder, would you be so distressed by the curve of the back of your arm, the shape of your butt, the fact there isn't a gap between your upper thighs? Not as likely. You'd probably be off somewhere thinking other thoughts about things that matter to you and enjoying life, free from the encumbering worry that your body doesn't measure up.

Be mindful of the things your eating disorder is twisting into negatives in your mind and distorting in your self-reflections. Your eating disorder can do this with any aspect of yourself including your body, personality, intellect, or any other aspect of identity. Not only can your eating disorder do this, it *will* do this.

If you are engaging in self-reflection and the highlight reel plays only negative things, your eating disorder is using negative filtering. Having awareness of what negative filtering is helps you to see it for what it is, a dirty trick played by your eating disorder. When you understand the process that's happening, you can choose not to buy in.

Others

NEGATIVE FILTERING your opinions of others can take shape in several forms but ultimately has one type of outcome; negative filtering has a corrosive effect on your connections, on your ability to trust others, and on your hope for a fulfilling, peaceful, happy future. Healthy, supportive relationships are necessary for recovery and for a satisfying life.

Negative filtering, courtesy of your eating disorder, can occur on an individual level. This was discussed in the previous chapter about discounting the positive, wherein you couldn't give your mother enough recognition for the positive things she does for you. Remember, negative filtering is complementary to discounting the positive.

In the example with your mother being a support for you, negative filtering is when you focus on the one time your mother disappointed you. Perhaps your mom needed to cancel your family therapy session at the last minute? Your eating disorder warps the reality using negative filtering. The reality is that your mom has attended five other family therapy sessions with you and continually demonstrates that she genuinely cares about your recovery.

However, when you look at this through the negative filtering lens, you focus solely on the single time she needed to cancel unexpectedly. Your eating disorder doesn't give her a fair assessment. Your eating disorder's yet again distanced you from a valuable, supportive person and has made you more vulnerable to eating disorder behaviors.

Negative filtering can occur on the individual level when the filter is aimed at a specific person. It can also take place on a broader level, where your eating disorder causes you to lose faith in people overall.

People support you *and* people let you down. This is a realistic evaluation of the incredibly complex topic of human relationships. Negative filtering, though, will cause you to think of the worst interactions you've had; breakups, people lying about you, betrayals, disappointment, and moments you've been abandoned. All those things are real but there's more to the story.

Negative filtering is concluding romantic relationships are wholly terrible because you've been through a difficult breakup. If you're having thoughts like "all people suck," you are falling victim to negative filtering. It's normal to think "all people suck" sometimes. I know I do, especially because my sense of humor is dark and hyperbolic. But, that's not what I truly believe overall about people. It's just a thought, usually one that comes up when I'm trying to be funny or when I'm feeling sad. I can certainly empathize with the sentiment that all people suck and/or all romantic relationships are garbage; however, it only acknowledges the negative. And that's not a fair assessment either.

Negative filtering doesn't give you an accurate picture and, therefore, isn't helpful. Negative filtering causes you to focus on the weak points of a person or your relationship with that person because your eating disorder desperately hopes you won't use one of the most powerful tools in recovery—human connection through relationships.

Treatment

As with negative filtering of others and relationships, negative filtering about treatment is an effort by your eating disorder to dissuade you from using a powerful tool in recovery. Your eating disorder can use negative filtering before seeking treatment, during treatment, and after treatment, particularly at a higher level of care.

Your eating disorder wants you to see treatment through a negative filter so you won't initiate it, you'll give up on treatment when it gets tough and you'll look back on the treatment you've received with a bad taste in your mouth. Avoiding starting treatment, discontinuing current treatment, and becoming resistant to the idea of going back to treatment when necessary directly align with your eating disorder's mission to keep itself going.

When starting treatment, your eating disorder will use negative filtering to draw your attention to the potentially negative aspects of treatment. Your eating disorder will remind you that treatment can be expensive, that it takes time, and worst of all, that you'll have to actually *feel* your feelings.

Even the process of feeling your feelings is distorted by negative filtering. In therapy, you will absolutely have to work through painful emotions you've been avoiding for a long time. But, allowing your emotions to thaw also brings positive emotions too, like hope, freedom, and joy, which you most likely haven't been able to feel much of with an eating disorder on your back. It's not all as negative as your eating disorder would like you to believe.

A similar scenario takes place while people are at a treatment center as well as when they look back on their treatment experiences later. While in treatment, my clients often voice how much they dislike both treatment and the recovery process. I have a deep level of empathy for this sentiment. Sometimes, recovery just plain sucks.

Note how I said "sometimes" in the previous sentence because it does completely suck *sometimes*. Other times, you're making progress, becoming braver, leaning into your power, building confidence, healing your relationship with food, radically accepting your body, and getting to know who you are on a level that can only be experienced through the recovery process. Those times count too.

The same applies to how clients often look back on their eating disorder treatment. Past clients of mine have gone to treatment at a higher level of care such as residential and had their eating disorders attempt to distort their views of treatment experiences.

One client comes to mind from an outpatient group I was facilitating, where she shared that higher level of care was "absolute hell." She described how hard it was to weight-restore, to have to follow a meal plan, to begin feeling emotions she'd cut herself off from before, and how she began family therapy with family members who were likely struggling with eating disorders themselves.

I can see how that would all feel like absolute hell; her eating disorder only let her remember the hellish parts. In reality, she also was able to weight restore, became medically stable again, made new connections and friends in treatment she still keeps in touch with, improved her relationships with family members by learning to set healthy boundaries, and not only discovered what her values are but began living her life in accordance with them. Amazing!

But her eating disorder kept her stuck on the negative parts.

When she was having a tough time at an outpatient level, her eating disorder reminded her "treatment is complete misery" with the help of its negative filtering. Because of this, she went through a time when it was hard for her to come to individual therapy or to group therapy, both of which she said she truly loved. This was her eating disorder's best effort at getting her off the path of recovery so it could keep itself going.

The Takeaway

SOMETIMES LIFE, recovery, you, food, others, and treatment can be negative, miserable, flawed, awful, and downright no-good. This is undeniable. Your feelings about all of these topics are understandable and valid. And, there is another side.

The other side of the story shows us that life, recovery, you, food, others, and treatment can be neutral or even positive. Remember, eating disorders hate nuance and flexibility, so your eating disorder wants to stop you from seeing the bigger picture, comprising the bad *and* the good. When your eating disorder forces you to see things through a negative filter, hope is reduced, frustration increases, and you're more vulnerable to keep restricting, bingeing, and purging.

11

CATASTROPHIZING

Ever have a time where one thing goes wrong but then gets bigger and bigger and more and more anxious or terrifying in your mind, like a freight train of worry-gathering inertia, speeding toward a fiery, blazing crash? Example: You left a ticket at home for a concert you're going to later in the evening. Realizing this while you're at work, you instantly start to panic.

Your heart beats a little harder. A gentle flush surges through your body, then thoughts begin to race. You think, "There's no way I'll have enough time to stop by my house before the concert. The traffic will be too bad. It'll make me late. I'll have to show up without my ticket and there's no way they'll let me in without it. My friend who is meeting me there will be so mad."

This is catastrophizing. Catastrophizing is when you overestimate the negatives or minor inconveniences, concluding that things will turn into the worst-case scenario. Eating disorders consider catastrophizing a favorite pastime, a holiday to be celebrated 365 days of the year. Catastrophizing is one way your eating disorder sends you into an emotional tailspin.

Essentially, catastrophizing is your eating disorder completely blowing things out of proportion. As you know, when you're flooded with emotion, especially anxiety, it makes it more likely that you will use eating disorder behaviors.

As aforementioned, catastrophizing and anxiety are tethered together. Biologically, humans are hardwired to hate the emotional and physiological experience of anxiety. Early in the evolution of the human race, anxiety kept people alive by making them aware of potential danger. Today, most people live in a drastically different world where, luckily, they don't have to worry about being eaten by some sort of big cat species.

The problem is that your brain and anxiety still function in a way reflecting life-threatening danger in a more evolved world where life-threatening danger isn't usually at hand. In essence, your brain produces the same kind of anxiety for failing a term paper as it would if you were being hunted by a predator. Your eating disorder preys on this. Though anxiety may make you feel so uncomfortable you think you're going to die, you are not. The following sections explore how catastrophizing unfolds regarding the four categories of food, self, others, and treatment.

Food

EATING disorders connect anxiety with catastrophizing, and what better topic to make you feel so anxious you could crawl out of your skin, than food? Anxiety is a branch on the fear tree and your eating disorder loves to make you feel afraid of food. If you're afraid of food you either, 1) won't eat it or, 2) try to avoid eating it, only to later binge on it. Both of these are eating disorder behaviors.

Eating disorders can produce unwarranted fear through catastrophizing about food in general or by vilifying specific foods. Let's look at food in general. With the former, your eating disorder will produce thoughts such as, "If I eat too much today, I'm going to gain weight." Of course, with eating disorders, gaining weight is always the worst-case scenario because, to an eating disorder, there's nothing worse than being perceived as "fat."

Your eating disorder is completely disconnected from reality here. Aside from the questions rolling around in my mind like, "What does fat even mean?" and, "Why is fat the worst-case scenario, particularly compared to global world issues such as war, human trafficking, poverty, and hunger?" food doesn't work like that. You can't gain a significant amount of weight from eating too much food on *one* occasion.

Moreover, weight fluctuates over the course of the day and week, and fluctuates on a person-by-person basis. Your eating disorder has taken eating food and blown the consequences out of proportion, taking them to unrealistic, impossible levels that falsely seem dangerous. This is all to keep you stuck in the vicious cycle where the eating disorder can keep itself going.

Eating disorders apply catastrophizing to *specific* foods as well; these foods are usually the foods that are on your eating disorder's "bad list." This is your eating disorder's effort to make you afraid of the food, so either you won't eat it at all (restricting calories) or so that it will become forbidden and, therefore, tempting, making it binge-worthy. Let's get specific with an example.

Cupcakes.

Cupcakes are lovely, delicious treats that are just for fun. And, though your eating disorder would have you believe otherwise, fun and cupcakes are allowed. But, your eating disorder will employ catastrophizing to turn the joy of indulging in one single cupcake into a full blown, red alert, end-of-days anxiety disaster.

Here's the play-by-play: after hours, or more likely, days of deliberation (should I, should I not?) you decide you're going to have a cupcake when you go to your favorite local coffee shop to work. You order it and eat it. You even enjoy it.

Then, after you're finished, the anxiety freight train leaves the station, gaining speed quickly. Thoughts race through your mind. "That cupcake is going to make me gain weight. I bet I'm already up two pounds. I've ruined the whole week. I probably won't even be able to lose it. What if I gain even more? I probably will. I'll be fat in no time. I wonder if people will notice. I can't believe I ate that cupcake. I'm totally out of control."

Time for a gentle, loving reality check. You ate one cupcake. Things will be okay.

Catastrophizing fooled you into thinking things were much worse than they were and that you were rapidly speeding toward dire circumstances. Catastrophizing is a brilliant move on your eating disorder's part. You feel so anxious about your food choices that you restrict to compensate. Numerous clients of mine have told me they ate one of their eating disorder's "bad foods" and restricted for days until their anxiety subsided. Alternatively, you feel so guilty about eating the cupcake that will inevitably result in your demise, that you think, "Screw it" and go on epic binges because everything's ruined anyway.

Though these thoughts might seem melodramatic, they feel compelling and real when you have an eating disorder. Eating disorders distort reality. You can cultivate awareness around catastrophizing, though, by checking out how likely it is that the worst-case scenario will happen. I've yet to hear of one single cupcake making or breaking someone.

Self

CATASTROPHIZING HAPPENS in relation to self as well. Your eating disorder can use catastrophizing in such a powerful way that you catastrophize about your decisions or aspects of your personality. Eating disorders will take any decision you make and blow it out of proportion to make you feel anxious and emotionally dysregulated, baiting you into using eating disorder behaviors. We'll talk in depth about emotional dysregulation later in the book.

You might choose to decline an invitation to go to a friend's birthday party. Your eating disorder catastrophizes by telling you that you're rude and selfish for not going, everyone's going to notice you're not at the party, that your friend is mad at you, you're going to have a fight, and your friendship might not survive. Catastrophizing makes the situation seem extreme and threatens the fate of the relationship to make you so upset you'll turn to restricting, bingeing, or purging to calm the storm of emotions.

I've also seen eating disorders catastrophize about dimensions of a person's personality. I had a client once who felt uncomfortable with her introversion. She was soft-spoken and shy but consistently made efforts to socialize and had several close friends who thought the world of her.

Her eating disorder, however, knew that being an introvert was a tender spot for her.

She would catastrophize about finding a romantic relationship, often sharing her train of thought in therapy and explaining that she didn't believe she could come across as confident enough to potential suitors, she'd never find someone to have a serious relationship with, she'd never get married, never get to have children, and would die alone with her cats (she also had a dog though). It may sound dramatic but to her, and to everyone who catastrophizes themselves, it can feel irrefutably true in the moment.

Because this client valued relationships and ultimately wanted to be in a long-term romantic relationship and become a mother, her eating disorder catastrophized by playing out the worst-case scenario for her—that these things wouldn't come to fruition. In this example, not only did the client feel hopeless about and afraid of her future, her dislike of her introversion deepened. Both these resulted in her bingeing in quiet resignation to soothe herself.

Others

It's easy to catastrophize when others are involved. Eating disorders don't like for people to seek support or connect in meaningful relationships. Being in relationships with others is an inherently vulnerable position. You're investing yourself in someone else and trusting they'll treat you as you'd hope. Your eating disorder knows you are vulnerable in relationships and will exploit this to make you fearful.

If your eating disorder has any chance to make you think someone is letting you down, judging you, or worse, abandoning you, it will take the opportunity. Your eating disorder doesn't want you to have faith in other people because it doesn't want you to get support. Your eating disorder might do something like convincing you your father is going to be disappointed in you for your grades this semester; in fact, not only will he be disappointed, he's definitely going to bring it up in an awkward discussion. And, he'll probably say he doesn't want to help you pay for college anymore. And he's going to tell the rest of your family about his disappointment. And they, in turn, will feel disappointed with you as well. The possibility of your whole family being disappointed in you would be greatly upsetting, and ripe for eating disorder temptation.

Another power play your eating disorder will pull out of its arsenal is to catastrophize an event, concluding it with the end of the relationship or the person leaving you. Early in my recovery, I remember my eating disorder doing this to me. Not many people knew I had an eating disorder and even fewer knew I was trying to recover from it.

Like most people with eating disorders, I carried an immense amount of shame about the disorder itself. Every time I wanted to take a risk and reach out to share with a close friend or family member that I had an eating disorder and was actively trying to recover, my eating disorder would not-so-gently remind me that eating disorders are highly stigmatized and the people I share with might feel that way as well.

I visualized what it would be like to let the next person in on my closely-guarded secret, rehearsing what I would say in my head. My eating disorder would swiftly interrupt and hijack the scene in my mind. It went something like this: I share my secret, scared out of my mind. The person I reveal my secret to is disappointed and repulsed. I imagined that they would leave after knowing my secret, either rejecting me outright after my disclosure or by slowly allowing our relationship to fizzle away.

Of course, none of these fears came true.

Eating disorders catastrophize about other people's reactions. Your eating disorder will make you think others will have the worst possible reaction to whatever it is you did or said. Often, the reaction you fear is that others will be angry, disappointed or critical. Not just a *little* angry or a little disappointed or a little bit critical, but highly angry, disappointed, and critical instead.

Catastrophizing tricks you into thinking the other person's reaction will be much worse than it's likely to be. Catastrophizing contributes to enacting unhelpful relationship patterns, such as withdrawing, which increases anxiety about relationships and results in isolating behavior.

Have you ever felt as though you were walking on eggshells? Sometimes, this feeling of being overly conscious of what you say or do for fear of a terrible reaction is caused by catastrophizing. If you are walking on eggshells, fearful that someone else will have a catastrophic reaction at any moment, you are not likely to bring up what you need. This is a dreadful combination. You feel anxious, increasing your likelihood of using eating disorder behaviors, and you can't get your needs met—which also increases the likelihood of using eating disorder behaviors.

Advocating for your needs can be hard. Some of my clients would say this is the most difficult thing they're learning in recovery. But, it's an essential skill. You might need to ask for something, tell someone you need them to change something, or perhaps tell someone to stop doing something.

Catastrophizing will make you think they'll react terribly, discouraging you from advocating for your needs, resulting in you isolating in feelings of loneliness and resentment about your unmet needs. Unmet needs then increase your chances of using eating disorder behaviors.

Treatment

ANTICIPATING catastrophic outcomes for treatment is commonplace with eating disorders. Some of my clients who were considering going to a higher level of care expressed that they were terrified by this because they did not want to lose their eating disorders. Though people desperately want to live life without their disorders, when that possibility comes closer, people are also deeply fearful of what it would be like to not have the eating disorder in their lives. Who would they be without it?

Your eating disorder has helped you to survive difficult feelings and difficult times in your life. They are forms of coping that eventually become unhelpful, so it's understandable how the idea of losing your largest coping strategy would be scary. You feel ambivalent. You want to recover *and* you feel afraid of what it would be like without the eating disorder.

Catastrophizing occurs when the eating disorder distorts your expectations for treatment. The idea that your eating disorder will be completely cured, and therefore gone from every aspect of your life, is false. This is your eating disorder talking. This is your eating disorder's fear. It's not ready to leave you. It just wants to keep going.

Treatment at a higher level of care is intended to provide intense, focused therapy for a significant reduction of eating disorder behaviors, giving people a solid foundation for the cognitive (thought) work and interpersonal (relationship) work that needs to take place for full recovery to occur at some point.

Treatment at a higher level of care does not completely erase the eating disorder from your life. This is the distortion. "If I go to a higher level of care, my eating disorder will be gone completely." The eating disorder is taking treatment and blowing the expectations out of proportion, by making you think your eating disorder will be eradicated from your life.

A more realistic expectation for treatment at a higher level of care is that you could greatly reduce your behaviors, get a solid foundation for the thought and emotional patterns you need to improve, and can help you begin to repair relationships and set up lifestyle patterns for life beyond treatment.

Your eating disorder can catastrophize regarding treatment by telling you that if you go to treatment, you'll suddenly be cured. It can also catastrophize by telling you that you will fail at treatment. In my practice, I've heard clients say on many occasions that one of their greatest fears about treatment is that they won't do well, that somehow treatment is a performance task.

Here, the worst-case scenario is that you will "fail" at treatment. I've heard clients share that they are equally worried they won't "recover enough," that they will "waste money on treatment if [they] don't improve enough," and that they are worried that they will relapse and need to go back to treatment.

Their eating disorders makes all of these situations seem like worst-case scenarios come true. They're not. More importantly, none of those things has happened yet; they are imagined nightmares. The fear of failing at treatment will hold you back from seeking treatment in the first place. This keeps your eating disorder alive.

Your eating disorder might also catastrophize about what treatment will actually be like. Your eating disorder has a vested interest in making you think that treatment will be the most miserable, awful, painful, torturous, no good, very bad thing you could ever engage in. The eating disorder is dreaming up the worst possible scenario.

Further, the scariest part of this distortion is that you won't be able to handle this miserable, awful, painful, torturous, no good, very bad treatment. You absolutely can. Your eating disorder is twisting the reality. A more realistic perspective is that treatment will be rough, gut-wrenching at moments. But, treatment can also be deeply healing, breathing new hope into your life.

I had a friend who bravely chose to go to treatment at a higher level of care. After she completed her treatment, I asked her how her experience was. Without a moment's hesitation, she said, "It was easily the best thing I have ever done for myself." She expounded to say, "I learned so much about myself and totally changed how I see food." This sounds like a best-case scenario, not worst, to me.

The Takeaway

CATASTROPHIZING IS AN EATING disorder favorite because of its ability to raise anxiety by forecasting disaster. Anxiety makes you more likely to engage in eating disorder behaviors as well as making you more likely to overestimate the potentially negative effects of your decisions, and less likely to seek support from your relationships or in a formal treatment setting.

The first step in working through catastrophizing is recognizing it's happening. If you're anxious about the outcome of a situation and your mind takes you to an ending where you have no friends, lose all of your money, lose all of your relationships, gain all the weight in the world and end up homeless, you're probably catastrophizing. The second step for working through catastrophizing is to challenge it by realistically assessing the situation, considering how likely those worst-case scenarios are. They are usually highly unlikely.

12

EMOTIONAL REASONING

Feelings are feelings, not facts. Emotional reasoning takes place when you assume your feelings are the truth, accurately reflecting reality. With emotional reasoning, momentary, fleeting feelings are considered true reflections of the reality of the situation.

In the moment, emotions can feel powerful, sometimes shaking you to the core. The distortion occurs when the power or intensity of the emotion is mistaken for the truth of the situation. Your eating disorder would like you to believe your negative feelings are true, that you are incapable of tolerating them, and that they're predictive of your future.

An example I often use with clients is with the emotion of hopelessness. If you recall a time in your life when you felt hopeless, you'll know hopelessness is a powerful emotion. It is both intense and painful. However, though you may *feel* hopeless, circumstances may not *be* hopeless. When you use emotional reasoning, you take your emotions at face value without considering anything else about the situation, allowing emotions to dominate your perceptions.

Emotional reasoning is dangerous. Like other cognitive distortions we've talked about, emotional reasoning clouds your assessment of your current circumstance and provides negative implications for the future. Your eating disorder will trick you into thinking the future is hopeless and your temporary uncomfortable feelings will last forever. If this were true and those temporary feelings did last forever, I'd understand why you wouldn't think recovery was worth it. Fortunately, the truth is that recovery is not only possible but totally worth it.

Here's the deal. Emotions are great. They are your data. They are your teachers. They deepen and enrich you. Emotional reasoning, though, exploits your emotions by taking intense, painful emotions and blowing them way out of proportion, driving you to faulty conclusions about the future.

Eating disorders use emotional reasoning to direct your focus to what feels bad, literally toward your emotional pain. Feeling overwhelmed by negative emotions and believing these are indicative of how your future will be, is an effective recipe for getting you to turn to your eating disorder for comfort.

Food

WITH FOOD, your eating disorder will convince you that your temporary negative feelings will remain permanent. In recovery, when you start normalizing your eating, you're practicing a different way of eating. This makes everyone feel very uncomfortable. Feelings of anxiety, dread, and frustration are common. Your eating disorder uses emotional reasoning by convincing you that normal eating will always feel dreadful and frustrating. I promise recovery does not feel like that.

One example of this relates to specific foods. Let's say cheese is one of your "fear foods," a food your eating disorder has previously prohibited. Cheese is a food you've become anxious about eating. In recovery, when you reintroduce cheese into your diet, your eating disorder will take the anxiety you inevitably and understandably feel about cheese, and make it seem permanent.

Your eating disorder will use emotional reasoning to make you think that eating cheese will always be a difficult, anxiety-producing struggle. Cheese, or whatever fear food, won't always be difficult to eat, though. It will get easier as you continue to practice integrating that into your life. One day, cheese will just be yummy.

Your eating disorder can apply emotional reasoning to food in general. Many of my clients worry and express how they feel discouraged that eating food feels extremely effortful. When you are recovering from anorexia or restricting, food can feel torturous to eat, at times feeling like you're forcing every single bite. For those recovering from bulimia or binge-eating disorder, eating food can be terrifying. The sufferer is trying to avoid eating too much and triggering the urge to binge and/or purge. Your eating disorder would also like you to believe eating food will always be emotionally difficult. It won't. It gets easier with practice.

Emotional reasoning about food is one of the quickest ways your eating disorder can dissuade you from pursuing recovery. Your eating disorder, with the help of emotional reasoning, produces such thoughts as *this is awful. This will always be awful. I hate eating.* Thoughts like those left unchallenged lead to follow-up thoughts, such as *food is awful. Recovery is awful. I don't want to do this. I can't do this.*

Here, you're absolutely set up to continue using behaviors, keeping the eating disorder going.

Self

YOU CAN EXPECT your eating disorder to have negative feelings about things that you thought, felt, said, or did. You may also feel bad about some of your traits, habits, or aspects of your personality. These are all common, normal human experiences. Sometimes you don't feel confident. Sometimes you feel regret. Sometimes, you feel self-conscious. This is all totally human, totally commonplace, and nothing to lose hope over.

This is where your eating disorder intervenes with unhelpful emotional reasoning. It tries to make you lose hope. As an extreme example, let's assume you're feeling particularly self-conscious. You recently went on several dates with someone you were interested in, and felt like the dates went well. You actually found yourself getting excited about where the relationship could go. Then, you got a text message from the person you were interested in. You scanned it. "You're great but it's just not going to work out." Of course, this person hoped you could still be friends.

Anyone who's gone through this knows how it can leave you feeling rejected, hurt, and perhaps even undesirable. You are emotionally vulnerable because in those moments you have uncomfortable feelings toward yourself—rejection, hurt, vulnerability. Your eating disorder will take these uncomfortable emotions and twist the truth. It will try to make you believe the feelings are true and will always be there.

In the case of being rejected by your romantic interest,

you feel self-conscious; emotional reasoning makes you think you deserve to feel self-conscious, and that you'll always feel that way. Being told you're not going to get another date is upsetting enough, but emotional reasoning adds on additional layers of upset, heaping on more negative emotions to manage.

Emotional reasoning makes you believe that negative feelings toward yourself are true and deserved, and further, makes you think they'll remain. This setup sounds hopeless. So, if things are hopeless, why not restrict/binge/purge? If things are hopeless, why bother with recovery? That's exactly the conclusion your eating disorder wants you to come to.

Others

YOUR EATING DISORDER will definitely have reason to use emotional reasoning with regard to other people. Sometimes, other people are difficult to get along with (as is everyone; again, no one's exempt). Sometimes, other people hurt us. All relationships have ruptures, points in time when trust has been broken, when something's gone wrong.

In those moments, you might feel devastated, hurt or fuming mad—or bitter or rejected. Instead of viewing this as a trying but unavoidable part of relationships, your eating disorder will take those feelings to obscure the truth. Emotional reasoning about others makes you think the worst of the other person, forcing you to believe that those feelings toward the other person are unchangeable and the situation irreparable.

Friends get into arguments. That's normal. Imagine that

your friend promised she'd help with something important, like helping you practice your interview skills for an upcoming interview for a job you've got your heart set on. You plan to meet to do a mock interview with her, but she cancels on you at the last minute. You don't have enough time to reschedule your interview practice session with her before your actual job interview comes around. You feel pissed. How could she do this to you? Her reason for canceling wasn't justified to you.

You feel disappointed. You were really counting on her, looking forward to the comfort you would feel from her support and encouragement. Now, with feelings of anger and disappointment, you make a judgment about her. She sucks. She's a crappy friend who doesn't care. Here, the truth about her quality as a friend is being twisted based on your momentary emotional reaction.

Emotional reasoning may take this one step further by making conclusions about the future of your friendship with her. Perhaps you're so angry and disappointed, you feel as though you'll never be able to forgive her for what she's done. This is making a permanent conclusion (not forgiving her) based on your temporary feelings (disappointment and anger in the moment because she canceled last minute). Emotional reasoning is sabotaging you, making things seem worse than they are because you are rightfully upset in the moment.

Emotions can feel incredibly intense, especially when they first begin to bubble up. Those emotions are real. They are valid. And you should value their input. However, there's also value in allowing yourself to evaluate the situation after the initial onset of intense emotions. It reminds me of when I've received upsetting or extremely annoying emails from someone. In those moments, it's understandable that I feel a surge of anger in my stomach. I recognize that anger and don't try to rush it away. But, I also don't send a reply to that email immediately. I would most likely be sending a reply based on temporary, intense feelings and it would be an unhelpful, sassy email I might regret.

Treatment

EMOTIONAL REASONING TAKES over both when thinking about entering treatment and once people are actively working on recovery. We've talked about how choosing any kind of treatment is a truly courageous decision. Even people who choose treatment, especially at a higher level of care, usually feel terrified before their treatment begins. Your eating disorder will use emotional reasoning to take your temporary, though intense, fear and try to dissuade you from going to treatment at all.

I've heard from clients—as well as from other clinicians —that the moment when clients walk into the treatment facility is the scariest moment imaginable in the clients' minds. I and other clinicians have had clients walk into the treatment center, feel overwhelmed by fear, and literally turn around and walk right back out the door. If you've experienced this, there's no need to feel embarrassed or shamed in any way. If you haven't experienced this yourself, there's also no need to judge. Let's explore why this event makes sense in the context of emotional reasoning.

The first steps someone takes into a treatment center are the scariest, most difficult steps possible. People are overwhelmed with fear, terror even, about what will happen in treatment; they have fears of being "trapped," and of the unknown. In this moment, I can wholly empathize with the staggering fear someone must feel taking their first steps into a treatment center. It would be completely over-whelming.

Your eating disorder will prey on this. Yes, it's terrifying, particularly in those first moments when the fear is at its zenith but your eating disorder will take that fear and twist reality. The truth is that treatment is scary *and* that's not the whole truth. Treatment is also awesome and enlightening and healing and even has moments of joy and fun.

Your eating disorder will take the intense, temporary fear from your first moments and try to trick you into believing every subsequent moment of treatment will feel the same. It won't. Your eating disorder would love you to walk out of treatment and never return based on the fear of those initial moments.

Eating disorders use emotional reasoning to exploit your treatment fatigue during various phases of the recovery process. Treatment fatigue is exactly as it sounds; you become emotionally tired from pursuing recovery. Everyone who has ever tried to recover has experienced this.

This is the fatigue you have to push through when you can't bear to eat another bite to complete your meal goals for the day. It's the sense of being tired of going to therapy, of talking about the same things. It's feeling frustrated with going to multiple appointments, week after week. Eating disorders like to take advantage of treatment fatigue.

Your eating disorder will convince you that treatment is exhausting and that recovery will continue to be nothing but exhaustion and strife.

It's true. Treatment is exhausting. Recovery is exhausting.

That's not the whole truth though. Recovery and treatment are also filled with excitement and victories and can be inspiring in a way that few other things in life are. Here, your eating disorder is trying to get you to give up, which is an extreme choice, rather than just taking a break or taking care of yourself, a more moderate choice.

Recovery is punctuated with moments of acute emotions. You can expect that, and you can take care of yourself by being gentle on yourself during those times. Though treatment and recovery can be painful, there is a bigger picture your eating disorder is blurring.

Know that your eating disorder will always try to make you believe you cannot withstand these difficult emotions and that those difficult emotions will persist, perhaps interminably. Your eating disorder is doing this to bully you into giving up on recovery. It wants you to choose to use eating disorder behaviors to soothe those difficult emotions instead.

The Takeaway

YOUR EATING DISORDER is always actively pursuing its mission to keep itself going, to keep you bingeing, purging, restricting. One of the most powerful reasons to use eating disorder behaviors like bingeing, purging, and restricting is to attempt to cope with uncomfortable emotions. Your eating disorder will try to get you to believe the uncomfortable emotions represent the truth and reality of your circumstances. Further, your eating disorder will try to trick you into believing uncomfortable feelings will remain, without any hope of remission.

Your eating disorder is working to disempower you, to fool you into thinking you can't survive temporary pain.

Your eating disorder wants you to give up. When your eating disorder is using emotional reasoning against you, gently remind yourself that feelings are feelings, not necessarily facts. Remind yourself that no one ever died from feeling an emotion. And, remind yourself that feelings come and—luckily—feelings go.

13

"SHOULD" STATEMENTS

Should statements are attempts to get ourselves, or others, to do something, to complete something or to be a certain way. With *should* statements, you think thoughts such as, "I should eat healthier," or, "He should be more supportive." *Should* statements are thoughts that contain "should," "must," or "ought," intended to get a desired outcome.

Should statements are problematic. When *should* statements are said to you, you feel guilt, and sometimes, shame. When they are said by you to others, you are sitting in a place of judgment and most likely imposing unfair expectations. When expectations are not met, everyone feels frustrated, and frustration that accumulates over time builds to resentment.

Eating disorders love to talk in *should* statements. *You should eat this. You shouldn't eat that. He should have done this. She should have helped with this.* The eating disorder won't miss a chance to *should* all over you. The *shoulds* are endless.

Should statements are powerful fodder for eating disorder temptation because they create guilt, shame, frustration, anger, and resentment, all of which are uncomfortable emotions your eating disorder promises to ameliorate. However, using behaviors to alleviate the emotions from such statements only leads to more anger, frustration, guilt, shame, and resentment from using behaviors themselves, e.g. "I should be able to stop bingeing. I should have recovered by now." *Should* statements are traps waiting for you to fall into them.

Food

EATING disorders produce endless *should* statements regarding food. *You should eat clean. You should only eat [x] number of calories per day. You should avoid carbs. Should, should, should.* Some therapists, myself included, will jokingly tell their clients, "Stop should-ing on yourself!" *Shoulds* are self-defeating and frustrating.

Shoulds trap you by placing unfair expectations from the beginning of an experience, making it near impossible to win. For example, "I should only eat [insert ridiculously low number] of calories today." Eating disorder *shoulds* make you feel you must comply with often unhealthy goals, where you're unlikely to be successful anyway. Of course, you're not "successful" in eating an absurdly low caloric intake; it's not sustainable and goes against your biological drive for survival.

Shoulds also trap you by criticizing things that have already happened. *Should* statements are the Monday morning quarterbacks of cognitive distortions. Your eating disorder will say you should have eaten a salad instead or should have skipped dessert. Well, Eating Disorder, too damn bad! I didn't choose a salad for dinner and I didn't skip dessert.

If you accept, without challenging, all the *should* standards your eating disorder carries, you will have countless things to feel guilty about. Guilt is a key contributor to eating disorder behavior and to relapse into eating disorder behavior once someone has made progress in recovery. Earlier in the book, you learned how your eating disorder wants you to feel bad about your decisions so you'll turn to it for comfort, continuing the vicious cycle.

Food is a perfect topic for your eating disorder to *should* on you about. Remember; no one eats perfectly if such a thing exists. Moreover, since you eat multiple times every day, your eating disorder has an abundance of instances to criticize. What a setup.

A healthy relationship with food requires you to have boundaries but to also be flexible when those boundaries aren't helpful. With *should* statements, there's no flexibility and most of the insight is after the fact, about things that have already happened and can't be changed. You ate dessert. Your eating disorder is upset over that. It's too late. It's a done deal. And, there's truly nothing worth worrying about here anyway. Accept it, be nice to yourself, and tell your eating disorder to stop *shoulding* on your food choices.

Self

SHOULDING on yourself isn't exclusive to food. Your eating disorder can make you *should* all over yourself for things completely unrelated to food as well. Virtually any category can become an arena for *should* statements. Several common categories to *should* on yourself about are work/school, your personality, and your body.

Eating disorders love to apply *should* statements to any

area including a performance component such as work or school. Many of my clients are students; though these students range from high school to college to graduate or professional students, they all have *should* statements in common. Their eating disorders tell them, "You should have studied harder for that exam," and, "You should have gotten into a better graduate program," or, "You should have more publications to your name." The list goes on and on.

With work, I've heard clients who are extraordinarily successful say, "I should be further in my career," "I should be making more money," and, "I should be better at my job." All these *shoulds* add up to feeling, at best, less than adequate and at worst, worthless or no good. When you feel bad about yourself, you are primed to use eating disorder behaviors to soothe yourself.

Your eating disorder can assault you with *should* statements about your personality as well. *You should be more social. You should be more confident. You shouldn't be so quiet. You should be quieter; people think you're too loud. Should, should, should.* It's particularly damaging when your eating disorder uses *should* statements referring to your personality because your personality is largely unchangeable.

If you're an extremely extroverted, talkative, gregarious person, it's not likely you'll be able to change that trait significantly. Perhaps you've tried to change it significantly, to be quiet when you truly enjoy being the center of attention, all because your eating disorder wants you to feel self-conscious about that aspect of yourself. You know how miserable that feels. Misery is an excellent reason to use eating disorder behaviors.

Your eating disorder will *should* all over your body. *It should be thinner. Your butt should be higher. You should have a thigh gap. Your boobs should be bigger. You should be more toned.*

Your abs should be flat. Should, should, should. It doesn't help that the *shoulds* your eating disorder conveys about your body are reinforced by the unending barrage of media images and articles promoting unrealistic body standards.

Let me draw attention to the word *unrealistic*. Unrealistic *should* statements means they're unreal; those images *are not real*. This is a perfect setup for your eating disorder, causing you to compare your body to images of other bodies that aren't real because they've been unrecognizably edited, Photoshopped beyond recognition. *Should* statements about your body create a direct connection to eating disorder behaviors. *My body should look this way, therefore I will use eating disorder behaviors to make it so.* Alternatively, *my body should look this way but I'm nowhere close so, screw it, I'll use eating disorder behaviors because I'm so discouraged and upset.*

Should statements are powerful weapons your eating disorder uses to undermine self-esteem and any positive feelings you have about yourself and your body. Remember, positive feelings about yourself and your body create recovery.

Others

YOUR EATING DISORDER can also *should* all over the people in your life. As with other cognitive distortions we've explored in the book, this is yet another way your eating disorder attempts to disconnect you from others.

Should statements directed toward other people have unique power in that they place you in a seat of judgment. I like to think of the judgment seat as a throne, like the Iron Throne in the Game of Thrones series. In theory, it seems pretty cool to be on the throne looking down on everyone else. But, the throne looks incredibly uncomfortable and represents how unattractive judgment looks when you apply it. When other people feel judged by your eating disorder's *should* statements, they want to disconnect. And, you yourself feel disconnected, which is extremely painful. Judgment is painful.

Your eating disorder can lead you to judge others' behavior. And your eating disorder always determines that the person being judged doesn't measure up. One common way I've noticed eating disorders will *should* on other people is by demanding that they should understand your eating disorder better.

Having an eating disorder is an isolating experience. It often feels lonely and the loneliness is present often, given that having an eating disorder makes you feel different, other than and separate, around one of the most common experiences people have—eating. Having experienced my eating disorder being wholly misunderstood by others, I deeply identify with how profoundly painful it is when other people don't get it. As a psychologist, I try to educate those who haven't experienced eating disorders. It's true that other people fall short in their understanding and often lack compassion.

However, keep in mind that your eating disorder will *should* on those who are already making an effort to understand. They should understand better or they should understand an intricate part of the eating disorder. Though that would be lovely, it's not necessarily realistic or fair. It's more likely your eating disorder is distancing you from the people who truly are trying to wrap their heads and their hearts, around this incredibly complex disorder.

One of the most vicious ways your eating disorder judges with *should* statements is by judging other people's bodies. This is the point in the book where you need to hold in one hand a heap of compassion for yourself and in the other hand hold unflinching honesty. With both, try to call to mind an example of when your eating disorder *shoulded* on someone else's body.

Every time your eating disorder looks at another person's body and determines it's not thin enough, small enough, or should be shaped differently in any way, your eating disorder is *shoulding* on that person's body. It is tacitly implying that person's body is not good enough as is.

With a heap of compassion in hand, gently use your unflinching honesty to ask yourself if your eating disorder has done this. Mine did, and I've yet to meet a client whose disorder didn't. It's part of having an eating disorder. This is yet another form of your eating disorder creating disconnection from others. Judgment is disconnecting in addition to being painful.

Treatment

EATING disorders use *should* statements about treatment. Recall that *should* statements are harmful because they conjure up feelings of guilt and shame. These feelings of guilt and shame arise from failing to meet unreasonable expectations. I've seen eating disorders paradoxically use a person's lack of progress to *should* all over themselves. I've had clients whose number one cause of relapse was feeling like they weren't recovered enough.

With those clients, their eating disorders would convince them they should be recovered fully, without struggles. And when this didn't happen, those clients beat themselves up and went on eating disorder behavior benders. *Shoulds* don't apply to your progress in recovery. You're at where you're at and that's exactly where you're supposed to be.

More obviously, eating disorders will use *should* statements to complain about treatment. Many times, I've heard my clients' eating disorders airing their grievances in session. Statements such as, "This should be easier," "You should tell me how to recover," "This should go faster," and "This shouldn't be so painful."

I hear your pain. I've felt that pain. Recovery really can be miserable. But, instead of seeking support and getting in touch with your grit, resilience, and determination, your eating disorder just wants to complain and make you give up entirely. You've probably picked up on this already, but your eating disorder is never going to be happy with treatment. *Shoulding* is merely one of many ways it tries to get you off track.

The Takeaway

SHOULD statements are a favorite eating disorder strategy to make you feel negative emotions about yourself and others. *Should* statements can criticize unchangeable things that happened in the past. This is incredibly unhelpful. *Should* statements can also set people—yourself included—up to fail by operating based on unrealistic standards. *Should* statements can be stopped by using acceptance. Things, and people, are as they are—not necessarily as they should be.

14

PERSONALIZATION

Have you ever been told you take things too personally? This is actually a cognitive distortion. Personalization is when people see themselves as the cause of a negative external event they are not responsible for. Taking full responsibility for something they were only partially responsible for is considered personalization as well. Essentially, personalization is when you bring yourself into the equation when the situation has little or nothing to do with you.

Eating disorders use personalization to manipulate in several ways. Eating disorders use personalization to cause you to feel responsible for things *you don't have anything to do with*. Underline, highlight, and draw little stars around that last part—*things that don't have anything to do with you.*

You might go to a family dinner that turns out terribly. The dinner is blanketed in the awkward tension of years of dysfunctional family dynamics. You think to yourself, "If I'd done this or never said that, dinner would have gone more smoothly." You know those kinds of dinners. We've all been to one.

In this scenario, it seems like those awkward moments would have happened, regardless of what you could have done. Your eating disorder is unfairly shifting responsibility to you in an effort to make you feel like you've failed in some way, or worse, to make you feel bad about yourself overall.

Your eating disorder can also use personalization to fool you into thinking you have control over things you don't. As an example, let's say that last night you binged and purged. Your body feels miserable the next day. When you go into work, your boss calls you into her office and tells you that your department will be restructured and the position you hoped to be promoted to will no longer exist. You think, "If I hadn't binged and purged last night, maybe this wouldn't have happened."

Here, your eating disorder is incorrectly connecting your bingeing and purging to the changes in your job. The restructuring of your department was going to happen whether you binged and purged the night before or not.

It's not your fault. However, if your eating disorder can fool you into thinking it's your fault in some way, you're going to feel much worse and be more likely to use eating disorder behaviors to comfort yourself. See how the eating disorder benefits from you feeling as if you're at fault?

Lastly, your eating disorder uses personalization to make you compare yourself to others, leaving you feeling less than. One way personalization comparison occurs within eating disorders is in body comparison. Eating disorders amplify our innate human propensity to make comparisons. Then, they combine comparison with harsh judgment, ensuring you'll feel like crap and as though you don't measure up.

With body comparison, your eating disorder will cause you to evaluate another person, like another student walking by you on campus or a woman walking through the mall. Your eating disorder will look at her, assess her, and draw a conclusion. The assessment goes something like this: "Well, she's not that pretty but she's got a great build. She's petite. Shorter and cuter than I am for sure. I hate being tall. And, she's definitely thinner than me in the legs and the thighs. Actually, she's pretty much got the perfect, toned, tiny little body I wish I had."

In this example, you conclude she has a better body than you. Allow yourself to call to mind a time when you compared your body to another person's, and your eating disorder determined that you lost; try to let those feelings come up. The feelings include sadness, unworthiness, and sometimes hopelessness.

So, how does this qualify as personalization? This falls under the umbrella of personalization because her body has nothing to do with you. Underline, highlight and draw stars around that one too—*her body has nothing to do with you.* Your eating disorder is artificially creating a competition in your mind.

In the best way possible, your body has nothing to do with her and her body is none of your business either. Pause here and breathe a deep sigh of relief. Thoughts such as, "Everyone on campus is skinnier than me," or, "All my friends have better bodies than I do," are your eating disorder putting personalization into action. See these for what they are. Let them go.

Food

EATING disorders can easily personalize things that happen with food. Your eating disorder would like for you to believe that other people are paying far more attention to you and your food choices than they are.

Personalization may take place when you go to your friend's house for dinner and to watch your favorite shows together. Your friend was nice enough to make dinner for the two of you and served you a big bowl of chili, topped with a thick layer of cheese. Your eating disorder speaks up again, saying to you "Of course she's serving you a fat portion because you are fat."

In reality, your friend was proud of the chili she made for your TV night in. In her family of origin, she learned to give big helpings of homemade foods because this was considered loving. Neither of these reasons has anything to do with you; she would have served the chili the same way to anyone else. It wasn't personal.

We can examine this example in reverse, so to speak. Consider the same setup. You are going over to your friend's house for dinner and TV, except in this example, your friend makes a salad with grilled chicken. Your eating disorder speaks up again, saying to you "Of course, she's serving you a salad and grilled chicken because you are fat."

Sound familiar?

Here again, we could look at the causes of why she served a salad. Perhaps your friend had a bunch of spinach in her fridge and chicken on hand that needed to be used before they expired. Or maybe your friend hadn't eaten many vegetables that day herself and wanted to get some in. Maybe she was simply struck by a grilled-chicken-salad-kind-of-mood. As in the first example, you can see that what she chose to serve for dinner very likely had little to do with you at all.

Eating disorders like to take personalization a step further by wandering into the land of magical thinking.

Magical thinking is characterized by creating false connections or relationships between things or events that are not related. Magical thinking is present in superstitious sports fans who have to wear the same jersey when they watch each game or they fear their team will lose.

Magical thinking in the form of superstitious sports fandom is nothing to be concerned over. But, magical thinking, specifically personalizing with food, is concerning. It emerged in the example at the beginning of the chapter where your job promotion was no longer available.

I once had a client tell me she ate pizza, which was forbidden by her eating disorder, and then her boyfriend broke up with her the next day. Her eating disorder personalized this by telling her what she did with food (eating pizza) was the reason why the relationship ended. In reality, her relationship was coming to an end anyway.

I've seen this same concept in a broader sense as well with clients. I've had clients who reported their lives were better when they were thinner and who thought their lives were going better when they were thinner *because* they were thinner. They felt sure their thinness caused the good things in their life. In fact, their weights and the happy occurrences in their lives were coincidental, the same way losing a couple of pounds and acing a test are only coincidence.

Personalization is a powerful weapon for your eating disorder because personalization makes you think you have responsibility in areas you do not, and often, cannot. By tricking you into believing you have more responsibility or power than you actually do, you will attempt to control things that are out of your control and you will feel bad when you do not get the desired outcome. Again, this is a complete setup for you to turn to eating disorder behaviors.

Personalization with food makes you think everything

that has to do with your food has everything to do with you. When you gently reality-check the circumstances, you'll notice that food and the things that happen in your life are less related than you think, if not completely unrelated.

Self

PERSONALIZATION WITH REGARD to self usually manifests by you taking a normal or common human experience and "taking it too personally," often forgetting that "your" circumstance is widely experienced by many other people. Eating disorders love to make you feel you're the only one.

One example of this is getting dumped. Every single person I know personally and professionally has been broken up with. Everyone gets dumped. Being broken up with is an overwhelmingly common experience, one that I'd argue is near impossible to avoid. However, when you personalize it, you feel as though you're the only person in the world who's ever been broken up with, that it happens more frequently for you, or that your breakups are worse than other people's. Even worse, you may believe—since of course, you are the only one—that something is obviously wrong with you.

Eating disorders can use personalization directly in an attempt to make you feel remarkably emotionally upset. One way eating disorders do this is with your weight. I've had numerous clients tell me that they felt like one of their body parts was "fighting them." I remember a client who shared that she was determined, willing to go to any length to get definition in her abs (a common eating disorder desire, and one that is culturally supported).

In her session, she explained that she felt like there was

a piece of fat that was "fighting" her on her lower abdomen. No matter what she did, what she didn't eat, or how she exercised, that fat remained. She interpreted this as her abdomen defying her. This was her eating disorder speaking, not her. Her eating disorder had convinced her that a patch of tissue was actually battling her, intentionally trying to wreck her happiness.

If we take a couple of steps back and look at this, you'll see that her eating disorder is taking a common experience of having some fat covering her abs and twisting it by convincing her that this section of fat is fighting her, out to ruin her happiness. This is personalization.

Her abdomen doesn't have its own thoughts, feelings, or agenda, but her eating disorder is personalizing it by making it seem as though the fat is out to get her. As an aside, eating disorders love it when you're at war with all or part of your body. It keeps the cycle going.

Others

PERSONALIZATION CAN BE EASILY IDENTIFIED in our relationships or interactions with other people. Recall that personalization is when you take responsibility for something that has little or nothing to do with you. When I think of the characterological traits of people who have eating disorders, I think of many clients who are conscientious, caring, hardworking, and conflict-avoidant.

None of these traits are negative. In fact, I think people who have eating disorders are often the loveliest, sweetest, most caring people anyone can come across, yet these traits serve as rich soil for personalization to take root.

What other people choose to do often has nothing to do

with you. Again, I mean this in a relieving way. Further, other people are entitled to have their own reactions, even if they upset you. For example, you may have a friend who's struggling with drinking too much. Ultimately, her drinking is her prerogative. She may choose to drink irrespective of whether you spend the day together and have a great time or whether you two get into an argument.

Personalization happens when you believe her drinking has something to do with you. It doesn't. Her drinking is only connected to *her* decision to drink, regardless of what is happening in your friendship.

I've heard clients talk about their parents, explaining they have a parent they feel isn't interested in them or maybe doesn't love them. If you have a parent who is not demonstrating interest in you or expressing affection toward you, that's on them, not you. It is a parent's responsibility to provide these things for their child.

For individuals with eating disorders, the eating disorder can use personalization to make you think your parent's indifference is your fault. It will make you think things like, "If I were [thinner, prettier, more muscular, smarter, better in some way, more successful, etc.] then my father would love me." The truth is, your parent's indifference is his/her own issue and you shouldn't have to feel like it has anything to do with you.

Your eating disorder has a vested interest in convincing you that things that aren't your fault actually *are* your fault for the following two reasons: to make you feel negative emotions, particularly toward yourself, and to create negative emotions toward other people.

When you feel negative emotions toward yourself as a result of personalization, you are primed to use eating disorder behaviors to cope with those feelings. Even more insidious is how your eating disorder can be used as a way to please others or try to gain their approval. I've worked with numerous clients who used eating disorder behaviors in an attempt to get an unresponsive parent to pay attention, to prevent a critical boyfriend or girlfriend from lashing out, or to make an ungrateful employer recognize their hard work.

In my own life, I restricted to gain approval from several close people in my life. I wanted those people to see me, to love me, and to meet my needs. My eating disorder used personalization to its advantage. When one of those people was being overly critical, making comments that cut me to the quick, I thought it was my fault. I thought if I was more of what they wanted—prettier, thinner, smarter, and so on —they would respond differently.

My eating disorder took their reactions and their criticism and made it completely my fault. According to my eating disorder, their reactions *were* my fault because I wasn't enough. In reality, the people I was trying to be good enough for had their own troubles that caused their volatile moods, indifference, and propensity for criticism. And, their moodiness, anger, indifference, and painful criticism would have happened regardless of whether I became good enough or not. After all, I've been good enough all along.

My clients who have used eating disorder behaviors in an attempt to gain approval, mostly by using behaviors to lose weight, had their attempts fail much like I did. Other people in their lives kept having their own reactions, kept being critical, or kept ignoring them. Their eating disorders continued to use personalization but changed the eating disorder behaviors they used.

After weight loss or improved job performance, or getting better grades and still having other people treat them poorly, those clients began to feel frustrated, angry, and resentful and subsequently, began bingeing or purging as a symbolic middle finger to that person. Their eating disorders would say things like, "I lost all of this weight so you would love me more. I spent hours in the gym. I starved myself for you! And nothing has changed. Well, fuck you!" And then they would binge and/or purge.

Sadly, yet luckily, we have no control over other people. You have no control over their feelings, their actions, and their thoughts, including whether they approve of you, notice you, or love you. It is key for you to recognize when your eating disorder is personalizing another person's reactions, so you can take a step back, get some perspective, recognize that you are not at fault and unburden yourself from feeling overly responsible.

Treatment

YOUR EATING DISORDER would love for you to take tough moments in treatment too personally. When you personalize things about treatment, you start to hate treatment. You feel discouraged. And, you may even feel bad about yourself. Treatment provides plenty of opportunities to personalize things that—remember—have nothing to do with you.

A common situation where your eating disorder will use personalization with treatment is when you compare your recovery to other people's or to a standard for recovery that you hold in your mind. When you think you should be "more recovered" or "recovering faster" than you are, you are most likely personalizing. Recovery goes at the speed it goes, and it's different for everyone.

Personalization can also happen when your eating

disorder compares your progress to another person's progress. This is common in treatment centers and in group therapy. Another person making progress in recovery *has nothing do with you.*

However, your eating disorder would love for you to believe that it does have something to do with you, that perhaps that person's recovery threatens your own recovery, or that you will not be liked by your treatment team as much as this other client. Negative emotions destroy connections with providers and peers in treatment.

Eating disorders love to lie to you about your treatment team's motivation. When your treatment team recommends you complete more therapy sessions or stay in a treatment program longer, you think, "Ugh, I'm so terrible. This is all my fault." Here, it's key to remember that *you are not your eating disorder.*

When your treatment team recommends more treatment, it means your eating disorder needs more treatment, not that you are bad. If your eating disorder personalizes this, you're more likely to feel upset and turn to your eating disorder to cope, undermining the treatment itself.

Eating disorders can also personalize dietetic recommendations. I am not a dietitian myself but I have heard clients share that their dietitian wants them to eat more of a certain food. They feel it's a slight against them. I remember one of my clients talking about how her dietitian recommended she start eating nuts more frequently, to incorporate more fats into her diet.

The client's eating disorder convinced her that her dietitian was trying to make her fat. Her eating disorder felt threatened by the potential addition of nuts into her diet. The eating disorder even told her that her dietitian didn't like her and that was why nuts were recommended. In truth, the dietitian and client had a strong relationship, the dietitian liked the client very much, and the recommendation for eating more nuts was made solely on the client's nutritional needs.

Your eating disorder likes to use personalization to make you feel bad and to distract you from your goals in recovery. If you're preoccupied with personalizing everything that is difficult in recovery, you'll be unable to fully focus on what you need to do in recovery. Personalization undercuts recovery.

The Takeaway

PERSONALIZATION IS a nasty cognitive distortion that's a favorite among eating disorders. When you personalize, you create false competition and comparison. When you personalize, you automatically feel responsible for people and things that have nothing to do with you. It's a heavy burden to feel as though everything has to do with you, that you have more power than you do, namely to control for others' reactions. By gently gaining perspective, you can see that you don't have to find yourself at fault and you can accurately place responsibility where it belongs.

PART III

Understanding Your Eating Disorder Using DBT

Dialectical Behavior Therapy

"Feelings come and go like clouds in a windy sky. Conscious breathing is my anchor."
-Thich Nhat Hanh

15

HOW DBT WORKS

Dialectical Behavior Therapy (DBT) falls under the umbrella of cognitive behavioral approaches to therapy. DBT was developed by Dr. Marsha Linehan, a psychologist at the University of Washington, originally for use with clients who had persistent suicidal thoughts.

DBT has been found to be consistently one of the most effective types of therapy for the treatment of self-harm, depression, anxiety, and eating disorders, and is considered the leading treatment for suicidality.[2]

DBT teaches clients dialectics—the synthesis of two seemingly opposite things. One of the fundamental dialectics of DBT is as follows: You need to radically accept yourself *and* you need to change. The dialectic is the *and*. DBT helps clients to simultaneously radically accept themselves while teaching them specific skills for creating change.

For example, if you feel overcome by feelings of inadequacy, DBT posits that you need to radically, wholeheartedly accept that you are not inadequate, rather that you are worthy, *and* that you need to use skills to soothe those difficult emotions.

DBT is a comprehensive system of therapy and when practiced in its true form contains several treatment components including individual therapy and coaching. The central therapeutic concepts taught in DBT are organized into four "modules": Mindfulness, Distress Tolerance, Interpersonal Effectiveness, and Emotion Regulation. DBT aims to increase mindfulness, build distress tolerance, increase interpersonal effectiveness, and teach skills for emotion regulation.

Each of these modules will be discussed in more depth in the following sections, relating them to eating disorder recovery.

Problematic Eating Disorder Patterns Explained Using DBT

.

16

MINDLESSNESS AND DISCONNECTION

Earlier, you learned that one of the four modules of DBT is mindfulness. DBT aims to increase mindfulness. Mindfulness, as defined by Dr. Marsha Linehan[3], is "the practice of being fully aware and present in this one moment."

In DBT, mindfulness is the concept underpinning all other concepts and serving as the foundation for all other skills to be built upon. Mindfulness is key in eating disorder recovery because it helps connect you to your body's needs and to your emotional needs. When you are not mindful, either by being mindless or by disconnecting from your physical or emotional needs, your eating disorder thrives. When you are not mindful, you are less likely to recognize physiological hunger and fullness cues. You are also less likely to understand what you need emotionally and use eating disorder behaviors to try to meet your emotional needs instead.

Mindlessness and disconnection are the opposite of being mindful. When you are disconnected from the present moment, you are not fully paying attention to what is going on around you or within you. You may feel out-of-touch with others or with what is going on in your internal world. I bet you've had this experience before. Have you ever felt like you were doing something on autopilot but you weren't quite sure what you were doing or why you were doing it?

This happens to me too every now and again. In fact, while writing this book I noticed I had gotten up and walked into my kitchen. Not until I was standing in the middle of my kitchen, did I realize I had wandered in there without much purpose. I stopped and asked myself, "Why did I come into the kitchen?"

When I paused to tune into what I was feeling in the moment (practicing mindfulness), I realized I'd gotten up from my seat and automatically strolled into the kitchen while I was in the middle of writing a chapter that was difficult for me.

Mindfulness offers a wonderful opportunity to better understand, and consequently, address your needs. In my case, I needed something to soothe me because I was having a difficult time with writing a part of the book. Wandering into the kitchen to find a solution is a holdover from my active eating disorder days.

Before recovery and without mindfulness, I would have walked into the kitchen and begun eating without questioning it, probably without realizing what I'd done until I was full of food I wasn't hungry for in the first place. As you can see in the example, what I needed wasn't food. I had an emotional need for comfort. When you identify what you truly need, you can address it properly, without having food or eating disorder behaviors serve as your default action.

Disconnecting you from your needs is a powerful strategy your eating disorder will use. When you don't get your needs met, you get upset. When your needs aren't met over a significant period of time, the upset worsens, often deepening into dark shades of resentment or hopelessness.

Further, when your needs go unmet for long periods of time you can lose touch with what your needs are completely. When I ask my clients, "What were you *really* needing when you used food?" many of them respond by saying, "I don't even know what my needs are. I have no clue." This is a result of being disconnected from their needs for far too long.

When you have an eating disorder, the eating disorder becomes the default, autopilot response for addressing your needs. This may take the form of eating when you're not hungry, eating to cope with upsetting emotions, not eating when you feel stressed or exercising when you want to escape painful feelings. Your eating disorder wants to keep you disconnected from those needs.

If you mindfully connect to your needs, you're going to discover that what you need is not your eating disorder. As you might imagine, your eating disorder is going to have a problem with that because it wants to complete its mission of keeping itself going.

In this chapter, we'll explore how to decrease mindlessness and disconnection and how to increase mindfulness so you can directly address your needs instead of using your eating disorder.

Food

IF YOU'VE EVER EATEN when you weren't feeling physically hungry or neglected to eat when you *were* feeling hungry, you've experienced mindlessness and disconnection. Eating disorders create disconnection from your physiological hunger and fullness cues. No need to shame yourself.

Eating disorders need to do this in order to exist. They cause you to gradually lose touch with how hungry you are so they can drive you deeper into restricting. Or, they subtly erase your ability to sense when you are full so you'll eat past that point, enabling you to binge. Mindful eating occurs when you are present in the moment with your body and food.

Connecting with your physiological hunger and fullness cues is key to eating disorder recovery. You have to be able to feel when you are hungry so you can eat, addressing your needs. You also need to be able to sense when you are full so you can respectfully stop eating when your body tells you it got what it needs. Your eating disorder prevents you from being mindful by disconnecting you from feeling hunger and fullness.

Your eating disorder also prevents you from connecting with how your body physically feels when you engage in eating disorder behaviors themselves. Your eating disorder has to create disconnection and mindlessness, otherwise you'd notice how awful it feels to use eating disorder behaviors. Let's examine this by type of behavior.

- Restricting: When you restrict, your eating disorder forces you to tune out your physiological hunger cues. The drive to eat is one of most basic yet vital human instincts. Hunger is its cue. If we don't eat, we literally cannot stay alive. This is not negotiable. Not eating is not an option.

When you skip a meal, your eating disorder does not

144 | RECOVER YOUR PERSPECTIVE

want you to mindfully tune into how much your stomach is growling. Instead, it forces you to ignore it. Hours pass and the hunger grows stronger. Your eating disorder doesn't want you to notice how painful it is to continue denying your body the food it needs to operate and survive.

Over time, the effort it takes to push the hunger out of your mind decreases as you spend more of your time disconnected from your hunger. Eventually, it becomes hard to recognize hunger at all. Your starving body, desperately in need of your help, sends you stronger warning signals, trying to get your attention. You might get headaches, have difficulty sleeping, or experience the cognitive fog and inability to concentrate that result from starving your body. As an aside, when your eating disorder starves your body, it's starving your brain too.

Your eating disorder doesn't want you to be mindful when you are restricting. If you were mindful, fully present and connected with that moment in time, you would notice that you were fiercely hungry, that you felt fatigued from lack of nutrients, that your head hurt and your brain wasn't working optimally because it was severely calorically deprived.

Using mindfulness when you are restricting would show you the reality of how you feel, not the numb, disconnected picture your eating disorder paints. And, you would be a whole lot more motivated to recover if you acknowledged how bad restricting makes your body feel.

- Bingeing: When you binge, your eating disorder forces you to tune out your physiological fullness cues. When you feel the sensation of fullness, it's your body's way of letting you know its needs

have been met. It's good. It's done. It's had
enough for the time being.

Fullness is a critical cue that informs you of your body's
needs. Fullness helps you know when to stop so you don't
overdo it. Consistently eating past the point of fullness, as is
the case with binge eating, doesn't make your body feel
good. You're giving your body more food than it needs,
much like filling your car's gas tank past full until it's over-
flowing. The extra is not helpful.

When you binge, your eating disorder disconnects you
from feeling fullness, the subtle kind of fullness you feel in
your body when you come to the end of a meal. It disconnects you from feeling overly full when you've eaten beyond
normal, end-of-meal fullness and have started to move into
feeling uncomfortably full. Your eating disorder even
manages to keep you disconnected from feeling completely
stuffed, as if you could burst, when you binge.

Many clients of mine have reported that when they
binge, their eating disorder caused them to be so disconnected from their fullness that they don't realize they're full
until they're so physically full they are in danger of vomiting
if they move the wrong way or are in terrible pain.

If you were mindful during a binge, you would feel how
physically awful it is to binge. You would notice how your
stomach feels tightly packed, how you have indigestion or
heartburn, how your stomach feels painful, and how you
feel exhausted and drained from pushing past your body's
limits.

Your eating disorder has to keep you mindlessly checked
out during a binge so you can continue to until you've
crossed the line into a full-blown binge.

- Purging: Your eating disorder uses disconnection when you purge. Though it's not uncommon for individuals who purge to describe purging as feeling good, most people report that at some point purging stops feeling good and starts to feel miserable.

When you purge, either via vomiting or through laxative abuse, it's forcing your body to complete functions that are normally for emergencies only. Vomiting and diarrhea are your body's version of a pilot pushing the "eject" button— because it is truly an emergency where no other options will work.

Your body is not meant to do these things routinely and the consequences of purging are steep, including digestive problems, electrolyte imbalances, and in severe cases, death.

I have a wild question for you. Have you ever purged mindfully? My guess is no. That's because your eating disorder doesn't want for you to acknowledge how miserable purging feels. Your eating disorder doesn't want you to be fully present in the moment when you're painfully forcing yourself to vomit or to notice how awful and painful your digestive system feels when you abuse it with laxatives.

Moreover, your eating disorder blocks you from being mindful, from being fully aware, when you make the decision to purge. If you were mindful in that moment when you're considering purging, fully in tune with the present moment, it might give you pause before acting. And, your eating disorder can't have that.

Your eating disorder continues to block you from mindful awareness the hours or day after you purge so you won't feel the purge hangover, that wretched feeling of exhaustion, low mood, pain, and emotional and physical emptiness. By preventing you from using mindfulness, your eating disorder stops you from connecting with the unpleasant physiological sensations that result from purging.

- Over-exercising: Eating disorders manipulate the power of disconnection and prevent mindful exercising. When you are mindful during exercise, you are connected to how your body feels. You can feel whether the movement you're doing brings you joy. You can sense the difference between working hard while exercising versus pushing yourself too far, past what your body is able to do.

Over-exercising is a favorite eating disorder behavior that would not be possible without disconnection. Think about the last time you did yoga, went for a run or lifted weights. Were you able to feel your body? Were you able to understand what it needed? I acknowledge that not every moment of exercise, even moderate, healthy exercise, is pleasant. But, your eating disorder takes the idea that exercise should feel uncomfortable and pushes it beyond what is normal. A great example of this is injury. Injury is different from normal, low levels of discomfort while exercising. Injury is your body letting you know something is wrong. When you are injured, you are supposed to attend to the injury. Your body needs you in that moment.

I remember a client who shared that during a time when she was restricting and heavily over-exercising, she went on a run on the treadmill but twisted her ankle stepping off the machine. She shared that instantly she was in pain and knew it was her ankle, not mild muscle pain from her run.

Her eating disorder swooped in and told her, "Get over it. Complete the workout! You have to finish this!" So she did.

She finished her entire weightlifting routine, including lifts causing her to lean on her injured ankle. After she finished with weights, she went into the next room and completed an hour-long yoga class. It wasn't until she couldn't ride her bike home from the gym, when the pain had become excruciating, that she was able to recognize how much pain she was actually in. The eating disorder stopped her from tuning into her pain just so it could burn all the calories it had planned to that day.

The relationship is clear. Mindful connection with your body would make it easy to see that using eating disorder behaviors does not feel physically good at all. Restricting, bingeing, purging, and over-exercising feel painful and exhausting. Increasing mindfulness, especially with your body, rebuilds the relationship between you and your body. When you are mindful, you can hear what your body is telling you and you can make the decision to give it what it asks for.

Aside from disconnecting you from your daily hunger and fullness cues and preventing you from truly feeling what restricting, bingeing, purging, and over-exercise are like, mindlessness and disconnection cause you to forget your food preferences. Your eating disorder can disconnect you from your food preferences so significantly and for so long you don't even remember what foods you like anymore. This is especially true when you have been following your eating disorder's food rules which kept many foods off-limits.

Eating should be a joyful, sensual experience in addition to providing you the nutrients you need. Without mindful-ness, you won't be able to tell what foods you like and what foods you don't. You also won't be able to tell what foods you like or taste good to you at the particular moment you're in. Let me explain both those points.

While I was struggling with my eating disorder, I didn't eat many cheeseburgers. My eating disorder thought they were all kinds of awful with the fat, meat, cheese, and the bun. I once went nearly six months without eating a cheeseburger, carefully avoiding them without drawing attention to my eating-disordered behavior. After all that time without them, when the opportunity arose to eat one, I didn't feel any desire to. My eating disorder disconnected me from the feeling I sometimes get where I'm craving a cheeseburger and a cheeseburger is the only food I truly want.

When I started eating them again, mindfulness let me know that I loved the taste of a good cheeseburger. I find eating them deeply satisfying. My eating disorder had clouded my understanding of my preferences via a long run of disconnection. At one time during my hiatus from cheeseburgers, I genuinely thought I didn't care for them. Clearly, I was wrong. The eating disorder confused me about what my preferences were overall.

My eating disorder also confused me about my moment-to-moment preferences. Though I know after mindfully connecting with my body, especially my taste buds, that I do, in fact, love cheeseburgers, I know I don't love them for every meal of every day. Our food preferences and needs change daily. There are days when a cheeseburger is the food I want more than anything else. And there are days when I know my body does not want a cheeseburger. It wants something else.

Understanding the daily shifts in food preferences is important. It can give you insight into what your body needs. For example, perhaps I don't want to eat a cheese-burger because I recently ate something similar and my body is asking for more variety.

Additionally, understanding the daily shifts in food preferences increases the joy you can experience from eating. Think about it; when you eat mindfully, in accordance with your food needs and preferences, the experience of eating is much more satisfying. You're getting what you want.

The opposite is true as well. I bet you've done this, as I have. There have been occasions when I knew I didn't feel like a cheeseburger, even though it's one of my favorite foods overall, but for whatever reason, I ate one anyway. Ever done that? Remember how the cheeseburger tasted that time? Not as good. It didn't taste as good because it wasn't what you really wanted.

This phenomenon is common in bingeing or mindless eating. If you've ever wandered into your kitchen when you were bored only to realize—half a bag of Doritos later—that you were mentally checked out the entire time, you understand exactly what I'm talking about. Keep in mind that your eating disorder always wants to keep itself going. An excellent way for your eating disorder to keep itself going is to trick you into thinking it can meet all your needs.

Your eating disorder disconnects you from what your true needs are and positions itself as the solution to any problem or remedy for any feeling. Sad? Eat something. Angry? Snack mindlessly. Bored? Binge.

The hard truth is that your eating disorder is never going to fully meet your needs. It's not going to meet your body's physical needs because it doesn't care about what your body needs. Your eating disorder only cares about its own agenda of keeping itself going, operating in reckless disregard of its negative impact on your body.

It also has no interest in meeting your emotional needs. It may seem like the eating disorder meets your emotion needs. Maybe you feel less anxious when you restrict or feel comforted after your binge, but in reality, it's only your eating disorder *partially* meeting your needs.

Using eating disorder behaviors is an attempt to cope. Your eating disorder may have even carried you through difficult times but it will never satisfy your underlying needs. And, it creates more problems, turmoil, and upset, all by virtue of you having an eating disorder in the first place.

Self

IN THE PREVIOUS SECTION, you learned how your eating disorder uses mindlessness and disconnection to prevent you from connecting with your needs regarding food. In this section, you will learn how your eating disorder uses mindlessness and disconnection to detach you from needs that are not related to food, such as emotional needs.

When you're mindful of your needs, you discover that often, what you need isn't actually food, though your eating disorder would like you to believe food or eating disordered behaviors will solve all problems. Your eating disorder would like you to stay stuck in a pattern of using food and behaviors as a blanket solution for meeting all of your needs.

We have physical needs that are not related to food. Your eating disorder doesn't want you to realize this. It doesn't want you to be mindfully aware so you can directly address your needs. It just wants you to continue to use eating disorder behaviors for everything, even when those aren't the appropriate responses.

Disconnection prevents you from accurately feeling how energized or how tired you are. Sleep is one of the best examples of a physical need that is unrelated to food. Your eating disorder wants to reduce your awareness around your need for sleep and rest. When you are physically tired, you are more vulnerable to using eating disorder behaviors. You don't have as much energy to use skills—rather than eating disorder behaviors—to cope. Further, sleep deprivation triggers increase the desire to eat past fullness, setting off the eating disorder vicious cycle.

When you are mindful, you are present in the moment with your body, able to notice if you need a nap or a full night's worth of sleep or if you feel restored and ready to take on your day. Sleep and rest are important needs for your eating disorder to distort. Getting enough rest ensures you're running at full capacity and that you have the most resources possible available to you. When you are fatigued, you are weakened. Your eating disorder loves how vulnerable you are when you are tired or exhausted. It makes it harder for you to fight off its advances and easier to resign yourself to using eating disorder behaviors.

For example, you work additional hours at your job, working upward of 10 or 12 hours per day. All day, day after day, you fight the fatigue. You try to ignore it, telling yourself to "power through" or to "suck it up and drink another cup of coffee." You come home late, around 8 p.m. and still need to make dinner for yourself. Instead of making a meal with all the foods your body is asking for at that moment, you order takeout instead and continue working through the night only to wake up the next morning and repeat the whole cycle.

Don't get me wrong. I have nothing against takeout or ordering takeout on a night when you're exhausted. But, if this is the result of habitually ignoring your need for rest that sets you up for emotional or binge eating, it is your eating disorder manipulating you.

It's true. You do need to eat dinner in the example. And, it also sounds like you need to reevaluate your schedule since it's so exhausting the only thing you're able to manage at the end of the day, most days, is ordering takeout.

Mindful connection with your sense of fatigue and energy inform you about how well the pace of your schedule is working for you. Or, it can tell you if the pace of your life isn't working, if it's too much or too fast. It's exponentially more difficult to make recovery-oriented decisions like resisting a binge, preparing a nice meal for yourself, or using your skills to self-soothe when you're feeling the urge to purge because you're exhausted.

You understand how difficult it can feel when you try to choose recovery instead of using behaviors. You need all the strength you can possibly muster for your recovery. That's why your eating disorder wants you to tune out your need for sleep and rest. Much like playing sports, if you play a tough opponent when you're exhausted, you're more likely to get dragged around the field.

Sleeping and resting are needs that energize and facilitate recovery. In the same way that emotionally eating when you're actually tired won't satisfy your physical needs, trying to address emotional needs with food will leave you feeling equally unsatisfied. The key concept is that your eating disorder wants to be the go-to solution for every need you have, so the lack of mindful connection with your emotions leaves you vulnerable to this eating disorder ploy.

I remember a client once telling me about a binge she had. She shared that she came home during the middle of her day following a tough grad school class in the morning, and needed to leave later in the afternoon for a meeting with one of her advisors regarding something that worried her. My client shared how she came home, prepared herself a meal, and ate. After she was finished with her meal, she found herself snacking on more food. Though the client said she didn't eat past her physical fullness, she felt upset by this experience. She couldn't quite put her finger on what was going on. She felt unsatisfied.

When we walked through the example, I asked her what she was feeling when she first got back to her apartment for lunch. She replied: "I don't know. I wasn't thinking about how I was feeling." I asked her to close her eyes and picture herself in the moment when she first got home, to allow herself to remember what was happening for her, to welcome any emotions she was having at that time.

My client shared that, after mindfully tuning in, she was scared. When she got back to her apartment she was scared because she was catastrophizing (see earlier chapter) about the potential outcome of the meeting with her advisor. She acknowledged that she genuinely needed to eat lunch but was completely disconnected from her feelings of fear, resulting in her eating disorder causing her to eat after her meal to address her needs. Here, she didn't need snack food for the fear. She needed comfort.

When you realize what you need emotionally, you can stop using food as the only answer. Even better, you can start *directly* addressing your needs. Once this client had the knowledge that she was scared, she had more options for getting her needs met. She could reassure herself by thinking encouraging thoughts. She could call a friend for support. She could tolerate and accept her feelings of fear until they naturally subsided. The options outside of food were—and are—limitless.

Mindful connection with your emotions not only informs you about your needs and gives you options outside of using eating disorder behaviors to address them, it also makes life richer. When you are mindfully aware of your emotions rather than disconnected, you live the full spectrum of experiences, seeing in full color and noticing all the details. This is similar to going to an art museum to look at paintings. If you are disconnected and mindless, you would walk by the paintings far too quickly, not allowing yourself to notice all the intricacies of each piece of art.

The same is true for your emotional world. When you're disconnected from your emotional life, everything feels blah and unimpressive, dull even. If you blow through your day without mindfully slowing down to notice the details, you're not going to be able to appreciate the nuance of that day, a day of your life you will never get back or have a chance to repeat. Mindful connection with your emotional life adds depth to your experience of your life and yourself.

In addition to reducing your ability to understand your physical needs and appreciate your emotional life, mindlessness and disconnection prevent you from pursuing your interests and passions. Sometimes, I think other people assume identifying and addressing their needs is all drudgery and hard work but many of your needs as humans are pretty awesome. You need things like food and sleep. And, you need to care for your emotions but equally important are your needs to pursue curiosity, to learn, or to create. Here, your eating disorder is trying to disconnect you from the good stuff.

Your eating disorder wants to disconnect you from your interests and passions because a life without passion, curiosity, and learning is boring, if not depressing. And, when life is boring or depressing, you're far more likely to turn to your eating disorder to escape. When disconnection pulls you away from the good stuff, your interests and passions, it enables your eating disorder to continue taking up space in your life. Your eating disorder would love to be the only passion you pursue. It would love to be the only thing you spend your time doing.

Disconnection from your needs prevents you enjoying all kinds of interests unrelated to your eating disorder. Maybe you want to learn how to crochet or paint or write or sing, or help rescue dogs... or write a blog, or build things, or create a new website. The possibilities are limitless if only your eating disorder would let you see them.

The catch is that you need to listen to that little "ping" of sorts that pops up inside you, almost like a kid raising her hand in class when she thinks of a great answer. Maybe you were that kid. Just like her, you need to attend to those needs. You have to recognize that you're curious. You need to use mindfulness to connect with your curiosity and passion.

The other reason your eating disorder keeps you mindlessly disconnected from these needs is because the things you want to learn or feel intrigued by, like learning how to paint, are usually great coping skills you could use instead of the eating disorder, during times of emotional upset. Writing, singing, building things with your hands, and gardening are all wonderful things to do instead of using eating disorder behaviors. However, your eating disorder disconnects you from the impulse to knit or paint, and from helpful coping. It wants you to turn only to it.

When you are disconnected from your need for learning and passion, your eating disorder has a greater chance of becoming part of your identity. In the same way that disconnection from your food needs results in you not knowing your preferences, disconnecting from your need for learning, passion, and curiosity results in you feeling like you only have your eating disorder.

Many of my clients over the years have described feeling like they "don't have a personality" or say, "I don't know who I'd be without the eating disorder." All of these lovely people, of course, have personalities—wonderful, interesting personalities in fact. But, continual stretches of disconnection from any pursuits outside the eating disorder leave people feeling lost.

Do you feel lost? If you weren't using eating disorder behaviors and your mind wasn't full of eating disorder thoughts, what would you like to learn about? Mindful connection with your creative and intellectual interests leads to experiencing your life and yourself in a deeper, more meaningful way.

Others

WHEN YOU THINK OF MINDFULNESS, you may think that mindfulness takes place when you're alone. Mindfulness, though, can also happen in interpersonal relationships. You can use mindfulness in your interactions with others, to feel fully present, increase gratitude, and become informed about your needs in the present moment. When you're mindful in your interactions with others, you are immersed in the present moment, not thinking of other things or waiting to move on to the next task.

Mindful interactions with others creates the best chance for feeling deep human connection. You are truly engaged with others in the moment, which grows gratitude. You've probably experienced a time when you were spending time with family or friends and were so engaged you didn't realize how much time had passed until you needed to leave.

Mindful interactions provide information about our needs with other people as well. When you approach interpersonal interactions mindfully, you are attuned to how you feel in that interaction. With mindfulness, you are able to notice how large social gatherings versus one-on-one interactions affect you. You notice how each person you spend your time with makes you feel. Perhaps you feel comfortable, accepted, and "seen" with some people more than others. This is all good data. It informs you of your needs so you can address them accurately and directly.

Your eating disorder prevents mindful interactions with others. When you have an eating disorder, your eating disorder becomes the conductor on your train of thought. Your eating disorder will disconnect you from being present in your interpersonal interactions in several common ways.

First, your eating disorder will force you to think only about food. It doesn't matter if your best friend in the world is telling you a compelling story about something difficult she experienced that week if your eating disorder is counting calories in your head. Instead of attending to your friend, your eating disorder distracts you with concerns about how many carbs you can still eat (or can't eat) today, by strategizing on how you can sneak away to the bathroom to purge, or by thinking about how much you will need to exercise once you get home.

Another way your eating disorder disconnects you in interpersonal interactions is by blanketing you in fears of judgment. Your eating disorder will plant fears in your mind such as, "I wonder if they've noticed that I've gained weight," or, "What if they notice what I'm not eating?" Both of these are incredibly distracting and disconnecting. The fear of judgment is a powerful tool for causing disconnection. After all, how can you truly connect with another person when you are preoccupied with worry that they're passing judgment on you?

In truth, people generally aren't watching what you eat and don't care about your weight. They are too concerned with their own issues, and some are more worried about how you might see *them*! And even if they do care about your weight, that is more likely a reflection of their own concerns rather than anything to do with you. You can let that go. Be gentle with yourself and give yourself permission to move on. It's their stuff, not yours.

Treatment

MINDFULNESS IS a cornerstone skill for recovery, especially if you are receiving DBT treatment. As we've explored, mindfulness can be applied to your relationship with food, to your relationship with yourself, and to your interactions with others. Mindfulness can also be applied to treatment, specifically as a means of informing you of how treatment is going.

I've had several clients say they have absolutely no interest in becoming more mindful about their treatment, often saying how "recovery sucks," and explaining that they don't want to feel more connected to the physiological and emotional discomfort of the recovery process. I hear you. I can empathize with that sentiment. *And*, I want to challenge you to incorporate mindfulness into your treatment. I want to challenge you to mindfully pursue treatment.

The opposite of mindfully pursuing treatment is being disconnected or mindlessly engaging with treatment.

Everyone has times when they're tired, overscheduled, and frazzled but if you come into every therapy session with no idea what you need to work on or how your week with food was, your eating disorder might be using mindlessness to sabotage your progress.

When you mindfully pursue treatment, you are aware of and attuned to your needs, including what you need from your therapy sessions. Mindfully engaging with treatment also means you've had multiple mindful check-ins with yourself over the course of the week. You've taken stock on several occasions throughout the week to notice how things are with your behaviors. Maybe you noticed that you binged more this week or restricted less?

All of these pieces of data are collected through mindfulness. Stacking your week with mindful moments, especially through journaling, provides insight about your progress that you can use in therapy.

Your eating disorder uses disconnection to sabotage your progress in treatment too. Just like those times you mindlessly approach your treatment, disconnection from treatment happens when you have no passion for treatment, or for recovery overall. When people are disconnected from treatment, they show up to sessions emotionally checked out, often having difficulty connecting with the purpose of the meetings. Sometimes, people start disliking their therapist, their dietitian or the appointments themselves— because they're already looking for something to dislike about treatment.

Disconnection is when you're not only not tuned in, but when you're just not feeling it. Disconnection in group settings might look like someone showing up to group but not participating or not actively listening to what their fellow members are talking about. Your eating disorder wants to keep you disconnected from feeling the desire to recover, from knowing what you need from treatment at any given moment, and from the deep feeling of attachment you may have with either other clients in treatment or your treatment team.

Treatment is just like other parts of life where you have opportunities to apply mindfulness. Incorporating mindfulness about how you approach treatment will help you to better understand, and—subsequently—address your needs. Mindfully approaching treatment helps to keep the passion for recovery alive when the going gets tough. Being present and mindful in your interactions in treatment, both with treatment providers and other clients in recovery, deepens the sense of attachment and camaraderie, an indispensable form of support.

Finally, mindfully approaching treatment means you are incorporating mindful moments during the week, helping you to create a practice of checking in with yourself and better enabling you to understand your progress. Taking a mindful approach will help you to get the most out of your treatment.

The Takeaway

THE TAKEAWAY MESSAGE from this chapter is to increase mindfulness. Mindfulness, as defined in DBT, is the practice of being fully aware and present in this one moment. Your eating disorder will always get in the way of you being mindful.

Your eating disorder would prefer you to be constantly disengaged from your hunger and fullness cues. It doesn't want you to feel how physiologically and emotionally uncomfortable it is to use eating disorder behaviors. Your eating disorder wants to keep you disconnected, floating through life and recovery detached from your body, your needs, and other people. Your eating disorder wants you to go on not knowing or ignoring your needs so you will continue to feel dissatisfied and use eating disorder behaviors to cope with the dissatisfaction.

When you're mindful with food, you know what foods you want and how much of them you want to eat. You understand what foods your body is asking for and have an overall sense of the foods you prefer and those you dislike. When you are mindfully attuned while using eating disorder behaviors, you recognize and can't ignore how miserable restricting, bingeing, purging, and over-exercising feel.

Expanding your use of mindfulness beyond food—to your understanding of yourself— helps you to learn about your needs, wants, and interests, which result in a richer experience of life. When you're mindful in your interactions with others, you acknowledge and attend to your needs and are able to be fully present in the moment, therefore making you feel a deeper sense of attachment to others.

Finally, mindfully approaching treatment allows you to evaluate your progress and ask for what you need. It helps you to show up to appointments fully aware and fully present, maintaining your emotional bond with other people in treatment and with your treatment providers, and helps to keep up your drive to recover.

17

EMOTIONAL DYSREGULATION

Emotion regulation is one of the four modules taught in DBT. Emotion regulation in its simplest terms is defined as "how to change emotions you would like to change."[4] The goals of emotion regulation are to "understand and name your emotions, decrease the frequency of unwanted emotions, decrease emotional vulnerability, and decrease emotional suffering."[5]

In contrast to emotion regulation, emotional *dys*regulation is characterized by a difficulty or inability to manage your emotions, often intensely experiencing emotions and then behaving in a way that is outside of what is typically considered "acceptable". When you are emotionally dysregulated, you are having big, overwhelming emotions and make decisions that are rash or out of proportion with the situation.

When you are emotionally dysregulated, the saying, "Your emotions have got the better of you," applies. Emotional dysregulation occurs when you're so angry you send an angry email back to someone before considering the consequences. It's when your partner says something hurtful and you threaten to—or actually, do—end the relationship impulsively. It's when you feel devastated by an unexpected outcome and hastily dash to the grocery store, buy all of your favorite foods, and binge. With emotional dysregulation, the emotional response is more than what's expected and the behavior used in dealing with your overwhelming emotions is unhelpful to you.

Everyone becomes emotionally dysregulated at times. No need to shame yourself. DBT emphasizes changing the behaviors associated with big, overwhelming emotions so you don't do something either unhelpful or that could have negative consequences.

Your eating disorder wants you to be emotionally dysregulated so you will impulsively turn to eating disorder behaviors to soothe yourself. Your eating disorder is invested in blowing your emotions out of proportion, making them feel bigger, more upsetting, and less manageable than they are in reality.

Through emotional dysregulation, your eating disorder drives you to act on momentary impulses to use eating disorder behaviors. What's worse is that after you impulsively use eating disorder behaviors, the temporary relief from restricting, bingeing, and purging will wear off and you'll feel bad about impulsively using the behaviors in the first place.

This is the eating disorder vicious cycle. Emotional dysregulation perpetuates the eating disorder by upsetting you and causing you to act rashly.

Food

INAPPROPRIATELY USING FOOD—AS is the case with restricting,

bingeing, and purging—is often the response to feeling emotionally dysregulated. However, your eating disorder can also cause you to become emotionally dysregulated about food itself. Ironically, becoming emotionally dysregulated about food also leads to using behaviors.

One way your eating disorder sets you up to feel emotionally dysregulated with food is by implementing rigid food rules limiting your nutrition and your fun, but these are also difficult to maintain in your life. One example of this is your eating disorder not allowing you to eat certain food groups. Here, let's use sugar as an example of a food forbidden by your eating disorder.

Your eating disorder doesn't want you to eat any sugar. Ever. If you do, you'll instantly become fat and your life will fall to pieces. The hard part is that sugar is ubiquitous and abstaining from all sugar all the time is impossible. Therein lies the setup.

You're invited to a friend's birthday party. At the party, there's alcohol (sugar), entrees with carbs (better abstain from those as well) and then, there's cake and ice cream. Instantly, your eating disorder throws an internal temper tantrum (because that's what eating disorders do). This is the eating disorder emotionally dysregulating you. Your eating disorder is offended by the cake and ice cream, saying, "Why, why, WHY is there cake and ice cream here?! That is HORRIBLE for you! I hate birthday parties. I should never have come. I hate everything. What am I supposed to do?! Eat it?!"

Yes, that's the idea. To eat and enjoy cake and ice cream for that special occasion. The rigid rules your eating disorder commands you follow make it extremely upsetting when you don't follow them. In reality, eating some sugar on special occasions is not as dangerous as your eating disorder wants you to think. But breaking such a "serious" rule causes you distress. It causes you to feel emotionally dysregulated.

One of my clients talked about how she "ate bad things" while on a camping trip. This meant she ate things her eating disorder didn't allow, normal camp food like trail mix, hot dogs and s'mores. Eating those foods on a camping trip is not a big deal. Her eating disorder didn't have the same opinion. Her eating disorder used emotional dysregulation to get her completely bent out of shape about eating these foods, forcing her to feel disproportionately upset about her food choices when, in reality, she had nothing to feel bad about.

For days after the trip, she restricted her food intake, feeling overwhelmed and disoriented by the massive amount of guilt she felt for enjoying the camp foods. She also exercised excessively to try to compensate for what she ate. The restricting and over-exercising were both eating disorder behaviors resulting from her feeling emotionally dysregulated.

Another example comes from a client struggling with bingeing and purging. She'd been working hard on reducing both those behaviors and was having some success. The days between each binge-purge episode were growing. One day, after a stressful interaction with her ex-boyfriend, she binged and purged. Her eating disorder manipulated this, blowing her emotional reaction out of proportion.

Yes, it is upsetting to use behaviors after a long streak of not using them but it's not the worst thing that can happen. Relapses and slips are part of the process. Instead, her eating disorder completely emotionally dysregulated her by making her feel guilty, angry at herself, and utterly hopeless about her future in recovery.

As she sat in my office bawling, she said she could never recover. She also said she had felt so hopeless, sad, angry, and guilty that she'd binged and purged multiple times per day. Her eating disorder took the normal upset and disappointment of having a slip after interacting with her ex, and blew her emotions out of proportion causing her to use behaviors to manage the difficult emotions; of course, this perpetuated the cycle.

Emotional dysregulation about food is a skillful setup on the part of your eating disorder. You're frequently interacting with food, multiple times per day or more, providing your eating disorder numerous opportunities to make your emotions about food seem unmanageable.

Luckily, because our opportunities to interact with food are plentiful, each interaction isn't as significant. One food choice will not make or break you. Being flexible and gentle with yourself when it comes to your food choices can help to keep your emotions manageable.

Self

IN THIS SECTION about emotional dysregulation and self, I want to discuss body image. Your eating disorder loves using emotional dysregulation to make you unnecessarily upset about your body.

Recall that emotional dysregulation is twofold: the emotional response is more than what's expected and the behavior used to deal with the overwhelming emotions is unhelpful to you. Your eating disorder will cause you become overly upset about your body and prompt you to use unhelpful eating disorder behaviors to resolve those feelings.

One way this happens is with weight. If you weigh yourself, please stop. I've never worked with a client trying to recover from an eating disorder who found weighing him or herself helpful. I've only seen it prove extremely upsetting. Weighing yourself allows your eating disorder to take an arbitrary, often inaccurate number with little meaning, and use it to ruin your day.

With emotional dysregulation, if you get on the scale and the number is higher, your eating disorder will create an extreme emotional response. You might feel infuriated, devastated, or immobilized by shame and disgust.

This response is out of proportion. And, I'm not saying this to invalidate your feelings. I'm showing you how the eating disorder is manipulating you. Your eating disorder makes you hastily decide you're not going to eat for the rest of the day or that you're going to purge to try to compensate for what you do eat. All this is because your eating disorder was able to get you worked up over a meaningless number on a scale.

Emotional dysregulation can happen with body image as well. If you look in the mirror and your eating disorder notices a dimple of cellulite or a shapely curve, your eating disorder is going to throw you into complete emotional chaos. It will cause you to feel the deepest, most painful shades of emotion you're capable of feeling.

When you're emotionally dysregulated about body image, your eating disorder's opinion of how attractive your butt is can ruin your day. When you recover *your* perspective, instead of seeing things solely through the eyes of your eating disorder, can you see how silly that is?

Emotional dysregulation about body image directly

results in using eating disorder behaviors. Your eating disorder makes you unnecessarily, disproportionately freak out about your thighs and causes you to impulsively restrict your calories, purge your meals or binge to punish yourself.

When you step back and look at the bigger picture, the flatness of your abdomen is insignificant. Other things matter more. Who you will see that day, what you will learn, what you will enjoy, and what things will challenge you? Those are the things that count.

Others

WHEN YOU HAVE AN EATING DISORDER, it's easy to become emotionally dysregulated about other people. Eating disorders are nosy. They constantly compare you to other people but what's going on with other people is none of your business. Please read this knowing I'm saying this with kindness and want to relieve you of the burden of concerning yourself with things that have nothing to do with you.

Comparison is the vehicle your eating disorder uses to drive you toward emotional dysregulation. With emotional dysregulation, your eating disorder will get you worked up over someone else's choices and cause you to respond to that behavior in a way that's unhelpful, by using behaviors.

Just as your eating disorder emotionally dysregulates you about your own body image, it will do that with other people's bodies as well. Your eating disorder constantly compares your body to other people's bodies. When it does that, you'll always come up short. Then, your eating disorder takes your emotions and magnifies them until they feel unmanageable.

For example, you're walking around the grocery store.

You look over at the woman at the end of the aisle. You scan her up and down and you notice she's thinner than you. And, she's buying cookies. Your eating disorder takes the opportunity to emotionally melt down.

You start to feel bad about yourself, ashamed of your body. You feel sad you're not the same size as her. And, you feel enraged that she's thinner than you and eats cookies. By now, you're completely worked up, so upset you could cry or punch something. You resolve to stick with your food rules until you look the same as her.

In that example, your eating disorder made something out of nothing through comparison. That woman's body and her choice to buy cookies have nothing to do with you. They certainly shouldn't hold enough power to ruin your day by making you emotionally spiral out of control. Your eating disorder followed things up by making you commit to restricting for the rest of your day.

Your eating disorder can concern you with other people's bodies and their food choices but your eating disorder can also get its nose in other people's business in other ways. Remember, eating disorders are nosy. Comparison doesn't stop with food and weight. Your eating disorder will use comparison to create emotional dysregulation in any domain. Common areas that eating disorders compare to others are achievement-oriented areas such as work, money, grades, and status.

Many of my clients are students. School provides endless opportunities for comparison, especially with grades. Comparing your grades to someone else's sets you up to feel inadequate because you need to earn a perfect score each time or run the risk of measuring up as less than.

My clients will mention how they find out someone else is doing better than them in school and how this is extremely upsetting to them. I've heard several clients say they were upset after receiving a 97% score because they knew someone who got 100%.

Their eating disorder causes them to be emotionally dysregulated, sending them into a tailspin about an excellent—almost flawless—97% grade. Sometimes, my clients tell me this turns into days of berating themselves with vicious self-talk, using eating disorder behaviors to punish themselves.

Emotional dysregulation from comparison to others is limitless and your eating disorder knows this. If it's not school, it could be your workplace or an organization you volunteer for or your church or your flag football team. Your eating disorder loves to compare, determine you don't measure up and flood you with overwhelming emotions.

In addition to comparison, your eating disorder will emotionally dysregulate you by diminishing your ability to handle feedback from others. Of course, there are instances in life when someone gives you feedback that's hurtful and unhelpful. But, there are other times when feedback, though difficult to hear, is delivered in a caring manner and is meant to help you grow. Your eating disorder doesn't like the idea of you growing, improving, and showing resilience in the face of difficult feedback.

Consider this example. At work, it's time for your bi-annual performance review. This is a standard practice and its purpose is to give you feedback about how you are doing. Your supervisor tells you she loves the work you are doing. On the company's performance evaluation form, you receive the highest ratings in 19 out of the 20 categories. This is a wonderful accomplishment you can allow yourself to feel proud of! However, you're not likely to binge, purge, or restrict if you allow yourself to feel proud or happy with your review.

Instead, your eating disorder enters the picture. Its agenda is to emotionally dysregulate you. The sole category in which you received critical feedback is where your eating disorder wants for you to focus, so you'll become upset. You were told that you could improve in a minor area. But, in an emotionally dysregulated response, you feel deeply wounded by this feedback.

It feels harsh, wounding, like someone scratching you on a sunburn. Your eating disorder spends the rest of the day causing you to ruminate on how wounded you feel, driving you to feel so dysregulated that it's difficult for you to finish your workday without crying at your desk. Of course, this leads to using behaviors.

Your eating disorder emotionally dysregulates you either by comparison—in which you never measure up and feel dissatisfied with yourself—or by making you hypersensitive to others' feedback. Other people can certainly be cause for upset; however, it's helpful to have awareness about how your eating disorder willfully distorts reality to throw you into emotional dysregulation, setting you up to binge, purge, and restrict.

Treatment

YOUR EATING DISORDER will emotionally dysregulate you about treatment as well. The eating disorder can do this in several ways. First, it can upset you over feedback you get from your current treatment team. Secondly, it can upset you about recommendations for a higher level of care. And finally, it can upset you over your progress in recovery itself.

Emotional dysregulation about treatment is when you become disproportionately upset about a treatment-related issue or recommendation and act rashly, either by using eating disorder behaviors or by disengaging from treatment.

Much like the earlier section where we explored how your eating disorder fragilizes you, decreasing your ability to handle feedback from others, your eating disorder also does this with your current treatment team and treatment plan.

For example, I once worked with a wonderful client with whom I had a strong therapeutic rapport. She and I had worked together for nearly a year in individual therapy. At one point in therapy, we began working on moving her through her ambivalence about recovery to fully committing to recovery. In doing this, we had to highlight in therapy the ways her eating disorder was not serving her anymore. We needed to deeply explore its harmful effects on her health, her life, and her soul without cushioning the truth with denial.

During one session, she shared that her eating disorder was getting in the way of her relationships. Not only could she not enjoy any social events involving food, such as going to dinner with a friend, but she constantly felt numb and emotionally disconnected from others.

I reflected this back to her, meaning I gently repeated what she'd just said aloud, verbatim. Instantly, her body language changed. She stiffened in the chair. She told me with an upset tone of voice that she felt that I was criticizing her for having an eating disorder.

For a brief moment, I felt blindsided. That was not what I was saying at all. I'd merely reflected back her own words. I quickly realized this was not my client, but her eating disorder speaking to me instead. Her eating disorder had taken what I said, the client's own words in fact, and had twisted them into criticism, causing my client to feel hurt, shame and rejection.

The client felt so hurt that she began to cry, and shared that she didn't want to finish the session. I gently explained what I thought was happening, that this was her eating disorder sabotaging our session by emotionally dysregulating her. After some deep breaths and a moment to process, the client softened, her posture relaxed, and said, "I don't know what happened. I got all emotional out of nowhere."

Her eating disorder did this to try to stop our session, to upset her so she'd go home and use behaviors, and because it disliked that we were starting to do deep therapeutic work directly threatening the eating disorder's existence. It wanted her to feel unmanageably upset and to impulsively decide to discontinue the session.

Another way eating disorders dysregulate you is by causing intense, unmanageable feelings about treatment recommendations. It is not uncommon for therapists, dietitians or other members of treatment teams to recommend that their clients seek a higher level of care or additional treatment. This might mean you need to add nutrition counseling to your week instead of only individual therapy. It might mean group therapy would be helpful as part of your treatment plan. And, it might mean that you need to seek treatment in an intensive outpatient, partial hospitalization, residential or higher setting.

When your treatment team makes these recommendations, they are doing it because they care about your best interests and genuinely believe more care is what you need. A treatment recommendation is only a factual piece of feedback; your eating disorder requires more care right now than your current treatment can provide.

Of course, you would feel upset if your treatment team is making this recommendation. No one wants to hear that they need to do more treatment, potentially interrupting their life to recover. But sometimes, there's no other way.

Emotional dysregulation occurs when your eating disorder has an emotional meltdown about more treatment. You may feel like crying or as if you want to yell, or feel so overwhelmed you can't find words to speak. Almost instantly, you firmly reject the idea of more treatment and adamantly state you won't go. Your eating disorder ruled that out as a possibility immediately after it was mentioned based on the intense emotions the eating disorder itself created.

Another way you can experience emotional dysregulation is about your progress in treatment. It's a bold move on your eating disorder's part to criticize your progress in recovery and it's a story I've heard over and over. Eating disorders are viciously judgmental when it comes to evaluating your progress, ironic as that may be.

Relapse especially is an area where eating disorders emotionally dysregulate you in an attempt to get you to quit treatment or give up on recovery entirely. All it takes is one tiny setback for your eating disorder to throw in the towel. It can be something as small as not being able to eat your full meal or eating something you enjoy slightly past physical fullness.

Instead of seeing small setbacks as normal, unavoidable, necessary parts of the recovery process, your eating disorder turns them into something much worse. Instead of feeling reasonably frustrated, discouraged, or sad about a setback, your eating disorder intensifies the emotion until it becomes unmanageable. And, in the moment when you've been knocked off center emotionally, your eating disorder says, "Forget this. Let's quit." This gives you permission to take steps backward rather than correcting course and getting back on track with recovery.

Your eating disorder undermines your recovery by emotionally dysregulating you about treatment recommendations, the feedback you receive in treatment, and about your progress toward your treatment goals.

The Takeaway

EMOTIONAL DYSREGULATION IS A POWERFUL, one-two punch to your recovery. Your eating disorder delivers the first punch by escalating your emotional upset until it reaches a point of feeling intolerable. Then, your eating disorder jabs by hastily driving you to behave in unhelpful ways like quitting treatment, acting out toward other people, or by causing you to restrict, binge, or purge. Emotional dysregulation sets you up to use eating disorder behaviors to relieve difficult emotions. This is all part of your eating disorder's goal to keep itself going.

As you learn to recognize when you are emotionally dysregulated, you can choose ways to cope with difficult feelings other than using behaviors. Cultivating emotion regulation skills is critical for recovery.

18

DISTRESS INTOLERANCE

Distress tolerance is the ability to tolerate discomfort or pain when the situation is unchangeable. Conversely, distress intolerance is the *inability* to tolerate discomfort or pain when the situation is unchangeable. Life and recovery are punctuated with painful times that serve as excellent opportunities for your eating disorder to sneak in. Building distress tolerance is critical for recovery and is a skill you can use throughout the rest of your life.

Your eating disorder disempowers you by leading you to think you can't tolerate the physical or emotional discomfort you're experiencing. When your disorder convinces you something is unbearable, you are likely to shift into your default habit of using eating disorder behaviors to cope.

Distress tolerance is necessary for situations that are painful but cannot be changed. For example, anyone who has lost a loved one knows that the grief accompanying that loss can feel debilitating. And unfortunately, when you lose a loved one the situation is unchangeable. There's nothing you can do to change the circumstances. You are left with the task of tolerating the pain of loss. Is it pleasant? Of course not. Can you live through the pain? Yes, you can. Effectively tolerating distress doesn't mean you like the situation or that you wouldn't change it if you could. Tolerating distress means you know there is no way to get rid of the pain and that your only option is to go through it.

Eating disorders like to keep people distress-intolerant, meaning they're unwilling to bear discomfort or pain. When your eating disorder convinces you that you couldn't possibly stand the pain of going through something, your first option of coping will likely be to restrict, binge, purge, or over-exercise. This perpetuates the eating disorder cycle.

Let's examine this more closely with an example. Imagine that you have a job interview later in the day. The job seems like a great fit for you and you hope you get it. You have two hours until you need to leave the house to make it to the interview, and the hours are unscheduled because you took the morning off to allow plenty of time.

As the interview time approaches, you notice your anxiety rising. You can feel your heartbeat speeding up as you think about the questions you might be asked. You notice your thoughts racing with worry about what will happen if you don't get the job. You feel sweaty yet clammy. Your stomach has that unsettled, queasy sensation.

Here, the situation is unchangeable. You can't move the interview time up. Getting the job will continue to feel high stakes; your eating disorder takes the anxiety and convinces you this is the worst feeling you could ever experience, that you can't make it through the anxiety, and the only option is to use behaviors.

Your eating disorder has taken charge and decided it's unwilling to allow you to feel anxious, even though the anxiety is temporary. You then find yourself halfway through a binge or starving yourself even though you need to eat lunch before you leave.

One of my former clients wrote the following regarding distress intolerance:

"Distress intolerance is a major part of my eating disorder—and it becomes a cycle. It starts with me wanting to avoid an uncomfortable feeling—usually judgment or inadequacy. Once I give in to my eating disorder, I am able to avoid the uncomfortable feeling or situation.

Then later, eating certain things or certain quantities becomes a trigger of more negative feelings—guilt, shame, disgust, personal judgment. To avoid feeling this way, I need to go back to old behaviors of restriction or limitation. I end up in a cycle of unhealthy behaviors and limited variety of foods in order to remain comfortable and avoid those unsettling, haunting feelings. I am acting on emotions, not logic. I can be more afraid of the immediate negative feelings than the long-term health effects of restriction."

YOUR EATING DISORDER's complete intolerance of discomfort keeps you reliant on the eating disorder for solace. Your eating disorder uses distress intolerance to make you underestimate yourself and your ability to weather tough times. When you think you can't handle things, you are set up to fall back on your routine of using the eating disorder.

Food

YOUR EATING DISORDER applies distress intolerance to your relationship with food. To start, we'll talk about distress intolerance with restricting and re-feeding. Then, we'll talk about distress intolerance with regard to eating fear foods and trigger foods. Finally, we'll discuss how distress intolerance interferes with your ability to interrupt bingeing and purging behaviors.

If you struggle with restricting, one of your tasks in recovery will be to eat more food, most likely both in terms of variety and quantity. Particularly for clients who are severely underweight, eating disorders use distress intolerance to make eating seem even more miserable than it actually is. In fact, your eating disorder's out to make you think that eating, and the emotional and physical sensations that come with it, are unbearable. It wants you to think you can't tolerate it, not even for a minute let alone for the many times you'll have to eat while recovering.

This is a lie.

In truth, increasing your food intake after long periods of severe restriction and starvation feel physically uncomfortable. Clients report feeling bloated, having digestive upset, and feeling uncomfortable with increased sensations of fullness. This is all in addition to the increased anxiety from eating foods against the eating disorder's rules, in quantities the eating disorder previously limited. It's important you work closely with a treatment team while trying to increase food intake and weight restore. What your eating disorder does to undermine your progress is take temporary discomfort and convince you it's unbearable.

You decide to eat a full meal your dietitian helped you plan. The meal is more than you're used to and has foods you don't normally eat. After eating, you feel "fuller" than usual. You even have some indigestion. Unfortunately, this is part of recovery for many people—temporary physical discomfort while your body adjusts to eating normal amounts of food instead of starving.

The eating disorder likes to focus in on the distress. It's going to draw your attention to any physical discomfort you're experiencing and tell you that you can't get through it or it's not worth pushing through. For extra fun and to make things harder to bear, the eating disorder will heap anxiety onto the physical discomfort, trying to get you to worry about whether this is normal, whether you'll be able to eat those foods, and whether you'll be able to recover at all.

Distress tolerance helps you live through the unchangeable discomfort of refeeding and weight restoring. *When you have distress tolerance, you can recognize that the physical sensations and emotions experienced in recovery are uncomfortable, not unbearable.*

Eating disorders use distress intolerance to discourage you from getting rid of bingeing and purging. If you've ever had the urge to binge and/or purge, you know that in the moment, it feels like it's the only thing you want to do. The desire to engage in behaviors is powerful.

I once had a client who was working on reducing her bingeing. She would promise herself to do it differently during her usual binge time. When that time in the afternoon came around, she felt overwhelmed with anxiety and said the anxiety was "the worst thing [she'd] ever felt."

When we talked about how long it was after the anxiety started but before she began to binge, she told me it was mere seconds in length. Her eating disorder used the powerful, intense momentary anxiety to provoke the client into rashly getting rid of it by bingeing immediately. The eating disorder completely disempowered her through this use of emotional dysregulation.

The lie the eating disorder tells is that the urge is so

unbearable you need to use behaviors to get through it, to make it go away. Eating disorders use emotional dysregulation to get you to binge and purge by making the anxiety— of trying not to engage in behaviors—seem much worse than it is, as well as by making it feel permanent.

Self

IN THE PREVIOUS SECTION, we talked about tolerating difficult physical sensations and emotions as they relate to food such as eating challenging foods in order to weight restore or tolerating the anxious temptation while riding out the urge to binge. Those examples specifically discussed how to incorporate distress tolerance with relation to food. In this section, we'll explore how your eating disorder uses distress intolerance to prevent you from coping with difficult emotions.

Our emotions are part of us. Emotions are normal and unavoidable. Emotions are necessary, providing information about how you're experiencing the world. Emotions can be pleasant, such as happiness, contentment, or hope, and emotions can be uncomfortable, such as sadness, anger, or fear. Humans are meant to experience the full range of human emotions and the ability to experience the entire range adds layers of depth, richness, and a grateful approach to life.

Naturally, your eating disorder isn't a fan of experiencing the full range of human emotion. Your eating disorder, through distress intolerance, convinces you some emotions are not as valuable an experience, that they should be ignored, shunned, and turned away from. Distress intolerance of your own emotions teaches you to fear certain feelings rather than wading through them and ultimately learning from them.

I often tell my clients that I think people have "go-to emotions." Go-to emotions are emotions are more comfortable for people to experience. Most individuals feel comfortable with happiness or other emotions with positive connotation. However, other emotions considered as existing more toward the "negative" end of the emotional spectrum, are harder to work through.

Even among those negative emotions, some feel more comfortable than others. Those are the go-to emotions. For me, it's easier to feel sad than it is to feel angry, while for others, feeling angry feels more comfortable than feeling sad, disappointed or shameful.

It is important to identify your go-to emotions so you know what feelings you're more likely to tolerate. Feelings that aren't your go-to emotions are the ones your eating disorder will prey upon, using distress intolerance to make you avoid them.

As I mentioned, these emotions are unavoidable. Recall how distress intolerance is defined as the inability to tolerate discomfort or pain in an unchangeable situation. Having uncomfortable feelings at various points throughout your life is an unchangeable situation. That's why your eating disorder wants you to hate them and become completely intolerant of them.

For example, let's say sadness is particularly difficult for you to feel. It is not one of your go-to emotions, so your eating disorder wants you to not only dislike the feeling of sadness but wants you to become wholly unwilling to experience it at all. This is a setup since sadness is unavoidable.

As long as your eating disorder has you fooled about your inability to tolerate sadness, it has reason to get you to use eating disorder behaviors. Every time you feel any semblance of sadness, instead of you thinking you're capable of weathering that tough emotion, your eating disorder tricks you into thinking sadness cannot be survived. Sadness must be rushed away with restricting, bingeing, purging or over-exercising.

Over the long-term, the emotions accrue, becoming backlogged and more difficult to feel your way through than if you allowed them in the first place. The following is a list of negative emotions common with eating disorder distress intolerance:

- Sadness: Typically experienced as a heaviness in the chest or as a hollowness inside, sadness can feel debilitating and is especially difficult when borne out of unchangeable circumstances. If you find out your best friend is moving away for a new job, you'd likely feel sad. This is completely understandable. The sadness is a reflection that the friendship was meaningful and that you'll miss your friend when s/he is not as close to you.

Your eating disorder, however, will use distress intolerance to make you think there's no way you can get through the sadness. Instead of attending to your feelings of sadness, acknowledging them and learning from them, you binge in an attempt to soothe yourself or skip several meals to try to numb the feelings away.

- Anger: Anger is often described as feeling hot all over, feeling a rise in blood pressure or the impulse to move, in some cases wanting to throw things, hit something, or yell. Anger is a valuable emotion. It gives us information about when our boundaries have been crossed. It lets us know when something is unacceptable. Anger has energy and power behind it. Eating disorders use distress intolerance to make you fearful of your own feelings of anger and to feel guilty about feeling angry toward other people. Anger is unavoidable, including feeling angry with someone else.

For example, one of your coworkers is assigned a task she needs to get to you by the start of the week. Despite sending her multiple reminders and offering to help when you realize she's unlikely to meet the deadline, your coworker gets the project to you two days past the deadline. Your supervisor holds you accountable, calling you into the office and scolding you for falling behind on the deadline. After you leave your supervisor's office, you're angry. Pissed even. You are mad at your coworker for dropping the ball and mad at your supervisor for unfairly holding you accountable for something that was not your fault.

Your eating disorder convinces you that anger feels too hot, too powerful, too out of control for you to handle, failing to recognize that like all other human emotions, anger subsides. When anger accumulates over time, it deepens and the roots of resentment take hold. Anger, like other negative feelings, is uncomfortable but not unbearable.

- Shame: Shame shows up in many forms, from the feeling of wanting to shrink away and hide from the world to feeling a hot flush of embarrassment. Shame is a universal, unavoidable human emotion. For most people, shame is hard to tolerate. It can feel extremely painful and vulnerable. Though difficult to do, it's possible to tolerate shame until the feeling inevitably melts away.

Shame is felt when we are exposed about something that we already feel vulnerable about. We feel shame when something touches us in a spot already emotionally tender. One example of this is body shame. You may feel self-conscious about your butt. Your eating disorder has told you for many years that it's "too big." While out shopping with one of your friends, she mentions her pants size which, of course, is smaller than yours. Your eating disorder brings up feelings of shame, intensifying them until you feel like you're going to bubble over with embarrassment. What a painful moment, and how mean of your eating disorder to pick on you about your body! Your eating disorder would prefer it if you believed the shame is too much to deal with. It wants you to restrict to get rid of the shame, purge until the shame is gone, or to say, "Screw it all," and binge. Your eating disorder says, "Shame is awful. I hate shame. I won't do shame, not even for a second. Why not use behaviors? We've got to escape this feeling. Now!" Though the shame is painful, it is *not* unbearable. It will pass too.

- Anxiety: Anxiety is usually experienced as a mix of physical sensations such as racing heartbeat, feeling restless or keyed-up, feeling nauseous or queasy, and your palms clamming up as well as psychological signs such as racing, worried thoughts. Anxiety is admittedly a tough emotion to tolerate.

Anxiety feels particularly aversive because it's tied to fear mechanisms from earlier stages in human evolution as a species. Fear used to keep people alive in the days when humans were in legitimate danger of being eaten alive—literally. However, these fear mechanisms remain just as strong in the present day despite humans' current circumstances being much safer. Most people do not experience life-threatening danger from predators on a daily basis.

Anxiety is a branch on the fear tree. It is valuable because it tells you that you should be concerned or that something's important to you. When you are waiting to hear back from someone you're interested in dating, it's natural to feel anxious. If you like them a lot, you might feel *very* anxious.

Instead of recognizing that the anxiety of uncertainty—not knowing whether you'll see your love interest again—is normal, your eating disorder uses distress intolerance to sabotage you. Your eating disorder tells you the anxiety is the worst experience you could possibly have. It tells you there's no way you can stand feeling anxious, not for another second. It becomes so insistent about its unwillingness to experience anxiety that it pushes you to impulsively use eating disorder behaviors. It tricks you into impulsively bingeing, purging, or deciding to restrict your calories.

Anxiety is hard to feel your way through but you *can* get through it. You *can* stand it even if you strongly dislike the experience. With anxiety especially, take deep, nourishing belly breaths. Breathe through it.

- Boredom: When I think of boredom, I think of the restless, unsatisfied feeling that comes from not feeling engaged, challenged, or connected enough. Boredom lets us know we are not getting

what we need or that we need a change.
Boredom is valuable because it prompts you to
change your circumstances. But what do you do
when the circumstance is unchangeable?

Boredom can be remedied with action but sometimes, a certain amount of boredom is inescapable. Think of a time you had to complete a task for work or for school on a topic you couldn't care less about. This is the unchangeable part. You find yourself wanting to do anything to escape or avoid this assignment. Your eating disorder whispers in your ear that anything would be better than the task at hand, especially using behaviors. Your eating disorder is so incredibly intolerant of any level of boredom from your assignment, that it refuses to do it. Your eating disorder says, "Let's go and mindlessly eat instead!" or, "Let's count our day's calories and calculate how many we have left."

Sometimes, things are less interesting than you'd like. Your eating disorder would have you believe that you can't push through boredom until it passes. Your eating disorder prefers it if you turn to it for relief from your boredom instead of having patience until circumstances change. One thing we can count on with life is that it doesn't stay boring for long!

Your emotions are part of you, part of your experience of life. Eating disorders use distress intolerance to make you unwilling to ride out difficult emotions until they inevitably remit. Your eating disorder does this to disempower you and drive you to impulsively use eating disorder behaviors.

Others

YOUR INTERACTIONS WITH OTHERS CAN, at times, provide you with excellent opportunities to practice distress tolerance. In the previous section on emotion regulation, we talked about how emotion regulation can help you to change uncomfortable emotions. With distress tolerance, we emphasize coping with the unchangeable feelings.

Difficult feelings caused by other people can be especially hard to cope with. You want the painful feelings to go away. Sometimes people try to get rid of those feelings by trying to control other people's actions. This is a trap.

Ultimately, we have no control over what other people do or say, or about their feelings toward us. The best you can do is to use clear communication to state your needs. It's up to the other person to respond. When they don't, distress tolerance is an invaluable skill to have.

Your eating disorder is not only intolerant of your own uncomfortable emotions but is intolerant of other people's negative emotions as well, especially when those negative emotions are directed toward you.

People in your life will inevitably think something negative about you. It's okay. It happens to everyone. Your eating disorder, however, wants you to believe that someone else thinking negatively about you is the worst thing that could ever happen, and that your emotions when someone else negatively evaluates you are unbearable.

The eating disorder setup works like this: Your eating disorder persuades you that other people's negative evaluation is awful. It tells you that you need approval from others. It tells you to avoid negative views of you at all costs, often resulting in you relinquishing your needs, stuffing your feelings, and engaging in copious amounts of people-pleasing behavior.

You live your life walking on eggshells, trying to be

everything for everyone at all times because someone else being upset with you is your eating disorder's worst nightmare. The subjugation of your needs alone creates a buildup of feelings making you prone to bingeing, purging, and restricting. Then, there's an additional layer of upset when this strategy inevitably falls short.

You truly cannot please everyone all of the time. The habit of trying to please everyone—anticipating their every need and twisting yourself to fit inside their outlined expectations—makes it feel more devastating when people-pleasing doesn't work out.

Let's explore this with an example to make things more real. When I was in school, I had a classmate who never seemed to like me. I'm speaking about one person in this example, though I'm sure there are others as well. I had several classes with this person and spent quite a bit of time with her. We came from different backgrounds and had different life experiences.

When we first started attending school together, I was interested in being her friend. I tried to be friendly and warm around her, inviting her to meals or events I was going to and offering to lend her books and movies I liked. No matter what I did, she never seemed to warm to me. Most of the time, she turned down invitations to spend time with me, she appeared unimpressed by my gestures of friendship like bringing her coffee or hot cocoa, and avoided me when we worked in teams on projects.

I couldn't figure out what I was doing wrong. So, I tried harder. My people-pleasing tendencies increased. I went out of my way to gain her approval by learning more about her interests and allowing her to make all the decisions about where to eat and what to do with our mutual friend group. She didn't respond. She continued to give me the cold shoulder. My anxiety increased. I obsessed over what I could be doing wrong, replaying every interaction in my mind, trying to find the error in my ways. Every moment I was around was wrought with anxious agony and laden with my desperate desire for her approval.

One day, I finally got up the courage to confront her. She shared that she didn't think I was awful but I wasn't her type. She told me she didn't think we had enough mutual interests to be friends, that she didn't like any of my interests and had no desire to learn more about them (especially sports), and she didn't care for my sense of humor. She said she couldn't picture us as anything more than classmates who were cordial.

I was devastated.

Flooded with sadness, shame, and rejection, I retreated back to my world of anxious overanalyzing, replaying every interaction I could recall in my head, looking for the ways I went wrong. I couldn't stand that she didn't like me. I'd tried so hard to be nice and to include her, going out of my way to learn more about her and her interests. And, she didn't like my sense of humor?! What?! I thought I was funny! What the hell.

This is the eating disorder setup. You can imagine how tempted you would be to use your eating disorder behaviors if you were in a similar situation. Your eating disorder wants you to use behaviors to rush away those feelings of sadness, shame, and rejection. It wants you to think you can't possibly stand someone disliking you.

I promise you that you can. I did.

The weeks following my chat with that classmate who simply didn't care for me were rough. It was difficult for me to allow those painful feelings to be, and to believe that they would pass. Every time I was around her, I felt that pang of not-good-enoughness. If you've ever been in a similar scenario, you understand how that provides repeated attempts for your eating disorder to bait you into using behaviors.

It might not seem like it, but it's easier to tolerate the painful feelings than it is to continue to use your eating disorder to avoid unchangeable, tough things. As much as it hurt me, that woman had the right not to like me and not to want to be my friend. And, I know I can weather the difficult emotions that come up in a situation like that. Those feelings are uncomfortable but not unbearable.

Another way the eating disorder ropes you into using behaviors with distress intolerance is by making you intolerant of other people's behaviors. Other people are going to do, say and think what they want and you have no control over any of it. Ultimately, they are responsible for themselves.

Don't get me wrong, if someone's being hurtful to you, it's probably helpful to stick up for yourself, state what you need, and try to improve the situation. However, there are times when that's not possible. Your eating disorder wants to make you completely unwilling to tolerate other people's behavior that you don't like. This gives you more to be upset over and, therefore, makes you vulnerable to using behaviors to cope.

People in your life are going to do things that will make you upset and that you can't change. Perhaps your best friend dated a total jerk. Your friend comes to you seeking support and is constantly upset by her boyfriend. Despite this, she continues dating him. And it continues to bother you.

Your eating disorder will use distress intolerance to deepen your feelings of upset, making you angrier about the situation. It reminds you that feeling angry is unbearable and after your friend calls you again to complain about her boyfriend, you feel so angry on her behalf and frustrated with her decision to continue to date him that—in a state of high emotion—you emotionally overeat.

Another example comes from the workplace. Imagine you have a boss, or maybe you really do have a boss, who seems to do everything the hard, inefficient way. Instead of using software your company has available for a task, she prefers to do it manually, wasting hours of your time building an Excel spreadsheet that creates more work for you in the long run. You've already addressed these concerns with her and she's decided to keep things "as is". You feel frustrated, furious and annoyed at her approach to work.

Your eating disorder uses distress intolerance to lower your willingness to endure the uncomfortable emotions. Your eating disorder wants you to be completely preoccupied with your negative feelings about your boss, and it wants for you to rush those feelings away through restricting, bingeing, and purging.

On a larger scale, your eating disorder uses distress intolerance to get you upset and unwilling to cope with feelings emanating from another person's addiction. Learning to tolerate painful feelings related to another person's addiction is one of the most difficult ways possible to use distress tolerance.

You can't stop your sibling from compulsively spending money on things she can't afford. You can't stop your best friend from engaging in her own eating disorder behaviors. And, you can't stop your alcoholic parent from drinking.

All these examples are extremely upsetting, perhaps some of the most difficult things to cope with. Your eating disorder tells you there's no way you can stand these behaviors and certainly no way you can survive the upset of being a bystander to someone else's addiction. But, *you can't control what other people do.* Sadly, this is also the case when someone else's actions are harmful to themselves.

Distress tolerance doesn't mean you never try to change things for the better. It doesn't mean you don't advocate for your needs. It doesn't mean you don't work to improve or repair when possible. Distress tolerance simply means you acknowledge you've met the upper limit of what you can do and that there's no room for you to change the situation. Things are as they are, as disappointing as that may be at times.

Using distress tolerance means you're choosing to allow negative feelings to come, and eventually to go, though experiencing those feelings is uncomfortable. Using distress tolerance means you know you can live through even the most painful, unchangeable emotions and that doing so is more helpful than trying to control other people's behaviors, trying to manipulate their opinion of you, and running back to the eating disorder when things get tough.

Treatment

It's possible you saw this coming, but your eating disorder is completely distress-intolerant during treatment. Your eating disorder hates treatment because it doesn't want to go away. The eating disorder wants to keep going. With treatment, you have to walk through uncomfortable feelings. There is no way around them. But, your eating disorder wants you to think you won't make it to the other side of these difficult emotions.

When it comes to treatment, your eating disorder is a quitter. At the first sign of something feeling difficult, it wants you to give up. It uses distress intolerance to convince you that you won't make it through the discomfort or that the discomfort isn't worth getting through. It can apply this basic principle to several areas of recovery including individual therapy, nutrition therapy, group therapy, and higher level of care.

In individual therapy, you have the opportunity to dive deep into the issues that initially caused and continue to maintain your eating disorder. For many people, there are painful issues connecting to the onset of their eating disorder and keeping the eating disorder going.

Clients of mine with histories of abuse have told me they believe that processing through the abuse, working through it in therapy, will be so painful they don't think they can do it. I hold people who work on their abuse histories in therapy in the highest regard. It's not lost on me how profoundly painful and trying it can be to explore those issues. It's one of the bravest things you can do.

What those people need to be wary of, however, is how their eating disorder will try to make them intolerant of working through those feelings. If it applies to you, those feelings will most likely be overwhelmingly painful and you can live through them, helping yourself to feel relief, to feel supported and more "seen", and to better understand how your eating disorder developed.

The Takeaway

RECOVERY NECESSITATES that you increase your distress tolerance. It requires you to build up your ability to get through painful or uncomfortable feelings when a situation is unchangeable.

Eating disorders like for you to be distress intolerant, rendering you unwilling to experience the slightest discomfort. This discomfort can take many forms including uncomfortable feelings and physical sensations with food, painful emotions and other people's behavior that is out of your control, as well as the necessary growing pains of going through treatment.

Your eating disorder tries to make you intolerant, unwilling, and resistant to experiencing any discomfort resulting from unchangeable situations. This is a brilliant setup. If the situation is unchangeable, you will continue being upset. And, if you're unwilling to tolerate feeling upset, you're going to have to turn to your eating disorder for relief, keeping the eating disorder vicious cycle going.

Recognizing distress intolerance for what it is enables you to make a different choice—to courageously wade through discomfort, knowing that it will pass and you will survive.

19

INTERPERSONAL DIFFICULTIES

One of the four modules in DBT is interpersonal effectiveness. Being interpersonally effective means you ask for what you want and can say no to things while maintaining self-respect and relationships with others.[6]

When you are interpersonally effective, you can get others to do what you want, are able to say no to things that don't serve you, and other people value your opinions. You're also able to work through change and conflict in relationships, and your relationships are strong and balanced in power. Interpersonal effectiveness sounds pretty great, right? That's why your eating disorder doesn't want you to be interpersonally effective.

Your eating disorder creates interpersonal difficulties. With interpersonal difficulty you're unable to ask for what you want, unable to say no to things you don't want, and find it impossible to work through conflict and change in relationships. Interpersonal difficulties will make sure you're not in relationships that are balanced in power and where both people are getting their needs met. Don't get me wrong; no one's completely interpersonally effective all the time, but when you have an eating disorder, your eating disorder wants you to have a disproportionate amount of interpersonal difficulties in your life.

It might be helpful to think of interpersonal difficulty as problematic when it's the overarching pattern or theme to your relationships, rather than just scattered, single instances. As I said, no one is wholly interpersonally effective and you can expect to have bad, difficult, and unsuccessful interpersonal interactions. This is different from *overall* having difficult interpersonal interactions.

When you think of your relationships as a whole—at work, at home, and with friends—examine the balance of power within them. If—most of the time—you aren't getting your needs met and you're experiencing a lot of conflict, or if you don't feel you have power in these relationships or can't say no to people, you're stuck in a pattern of interpersonal difficulty.

When your eating disorder has you stuck in a pattern of interpersonal difficulty, you're vulnerable to using eating disorder behaviors. Interpersonal difficulty means that you are not getting your needs met which is upsetting. It means that you're also unable to say no so you're probably overwhelmed from taking on too many things. The stress of feeling constantly overwhelmed by responsibilities can serve as a trigger for turning to behaviors.

When other people have learned not to listen to your opinions, you feel unheard. That hurts. And, it's triggering. When you're involved in relationships where there is a significant power imbalance or where another person has far more power than you, your needs won't be met as often. Finally, inability to work through change in relationships and get through conflict with other people is incredibly triggering.

By recognizing where your eating disorder is creating interpersonal difficulties, you can learn skills to increase your interpersonal effectiveness, helping you to get your needs met and strengthening your relationships. In the following sections, we'll explore how your eating disorder creates interpersonal difficulties in relation to the four categories of Food, Self, Others, and Treatment.

Food

Your eating disorder loves to create interpersonal difficulties with others involving food. Many people with eating disorders have a great deal of difficulty navigating their interactions with other people wherever food might be involved. This is great news for your eating disorder since food is a huge component of our culture and a daily need. Food and socializing are inextricably intertwined. By interfering with your relationships, it's interfering with your choices with food.

One component of being interpersonally effective is being able to ask for what you need in a way others can hear. In the chapter about mindlessness and disconnection, you saw how mindful connection with your body informs you about what you need in terms of food. Once you're connected to your needs, the next step is to take action to get those needs met. Let's work this through with an example.

One of your friends wants to meet up for dinner. She suggests you two go to a local restaurant known for its burgers and fries. Though these foods sound incredible to you, you also have a feeling that right now they wouldn't be great choices. Fries are among your biggest binge foods and you've recently had a tough week trying not to binge. When you check in with yourself about what you really need, you realize you need to go to a restaurant that serves food that's less triggering and more neutral to you.

Your eating disorder steps in, telling you that asking to go to a different restaurant is selfish of you. It makes you worry what your friend will think. It says you'll come across as high-maintenance if you suggest going somewhere else.

Without challenging this by bringing up your needs with your friend, you'll wind up going to the restaurant and will either have a harder time enjoying yourself in the moment because the food is triggering, and/or you'll binge later from sitting around your trigger foods for an entire meal. Your eating disorder wants to create interpersonal difficulties for you by discouraging you from assertively bringing up your needs about food.

Another way interpersonal difficulty manifests in social situations with food is by preventing you from saying no to foods you don't want or need. I'm sure you can remember a time when you were offered food you didn't want. Maybe you felt too guilty to say no in the first place. Perhaps you did politely say no but the person insisted. I've heard this referred to as "food pushing."

One of my former clients shared that she had a roommate who was "a total food pusher." She'd often come home to find that her roommate had baked cookies or other treats. Her roommate loved baking and was well-intentioned about wanting to share the sweets with my client.

My client struggled with saying no to her roommate. Her eating disorder told her it would be rude to say no, making her feel guilty. Sometimes, she'd be assertive and say no but when that happened, her roommate would insist, pressuring her several times to take a cookie. My client would end up eating triggering foods she didn't truly want which would either result in her bingeing or restricting to compensate. Her eating disorder convinced her to give up and resign herself to eating food she didn't want because she didn't want to upset her roommate.

My client and I talked about this in therapy, concluding she needed to have a conversation with her roommate about the "food pushing." My client was very brave and used her interpersonal effectiveness skills to have a separate conversation when she was not being offered treats to talk with her roommate about the impact of her food pushing.

My client's roommate had no idea she was unintentionally creating a huge struggle for my client and agreed to not "push food" around my client. And, from that conversation on, her roommate didn't. My client shared her relief at finding out that bringing up her needs with her roommate was okay; no one got upset with her for doing so and by being interpersonally effective in this way, she eliminated one of the major triggering situations she previously had to battle.

Asking for what you need with food is key in being interpersonally effective. When you ask for what you need and say no to what you don't, you'll greatly reduce the number of times you're triggered, making you less likely to use eating disorder behaviors.

Self

PART OF BUILDING your interpersonal effectiveness skills is through examining, challenging, and changing unhelpful beliefs about yourself or about how interpersonal interactions are supposed to work. These beliefs fit into the "self" category because they are your own, existing within you. In the next section, we'll discuss how your eating disorder creates interpersonal difficulty in actual interactions with other people.

We often carry deep-seated, unhelpful beliefs about ourselves and relationships. Your eating disorder is aware these unhelpful beliefs are lurking under the surface. Your eating disorder will take advantage of your unhelpful beliefs in an effort to create interpersonal difficulties.

One common unhelpful belief your eating disorder uses to undermine your interpersonal effectiveness is that your needs are less valuable than those of others. Your eating disorder prefers it if you always give up your needs. When your needs aren't getting met, you feel upset, resulting in difficulties in relationships. Not getting your needs met is also frustrating, discouraging, and sometimes feels defeating.

When you constantly allow other people to make the final decision—whether it's about where you go for lunch, right through to larger life decisions like where to purchase a home—you are giving up your power. Allowing others to choose for you or to overrule your decisions will lead to you feeling unseen, unheard, and neglected in your relationships.

In a similar vein is another common unhelpful belief your eating disorder exploits; this is that other people should already *know* what you need. It would be a lovely world if other people could completely understand and anticipate what you need. Unfortunately, that's just not the world we have to live in.

Even people you're close to and who know you well aren't able to know your every need at every moment. Your eating disorder creates the expectation they should be able to, though. This is a trap. No one, not even your loved one, is a mind reader.

When your eating disorder makes you believe everyone should already know and act in accordance with your needs, it's setting an impossibly high standard. And, it is setting you up to feel unnecessarily frustrated, angry, and disappointed with others.

If we reverse the situation, I'm sure you'd recognize that it would be incredibly unfair of someone else to expect you to know and attend to all their needs, especially their unstated needs. Likewise, it's incredibly unfair of your eating disorder to place this expectation on others. As annoying and exhausting as it may be at times, you have to be willing to ask for what you need. No one can read minds.

One more way your eating disorder creates interpersonal difficulties is by leading you to believe if you don't get the outcome you want with another person, it's all your fault. Your eating disorder does this to blame you when don't get what you want. This is to upset you which primes you to use behaviors and discourages you from bringing your needs up in the future. When you ask for something from another person, the only part you have control over is how and what you ask for. You don't have control over their reaction.

Believing you're solely responsible for the outcome of a request inaccurately relieves the other person of any responsibility. We've explored in earlier sections of this book how your eating disorder has a habit of trying to make you feel responsible for things that, in reality, you can't be responsible for.

For example, you could ask your boss for something in the kindest, most assertive, articulate way possible and your boss could still turn down your request. In this example, you did your due diligence. You asked with kindness at a good time and remained assertive about what you needed. But, your eating disorder keeps you bound to the belief that you should have had 100% control over what your boss decided. The eating disorder says, "If you would've just asked better, you could have gotten what you wanted."

Disappointing news it may be, but people truly don't always get what they want. And, that's *okay*. You can live through those instances. By building interpersonal effectiveness, you can continue bringing up your needs even if they aren't met every time instead of buying into unhelpful beliefs that create interpersonal difficulties.

Others

IN THIS SECTION, we'll discuss interpersonal effectiveness in your interactions with other people. Your eating disorder tries to create interpersonal difficulties for you in several ways including avoiding conflict, allowing resentments to build up, keeping you in relationships that need to end, and by preventing you from forming new relationships. All these forms of interpersonal difficulties set you up to frequently experience emotional upset, resulting in you feeling consistently tempted to restrict, binge, or purge.

One of the primary ways your eating disorder creates interpersonal difficulties for you is by causing you to avoid conflict. Admittedly, most people aren't thrilled by the prospect of conflict with another person, be that in the form of awkward, unspoken tension when you're together, making passive-aggressive remarks to each other, or by arguing outright. It's understandable why most people feel uncomfortable addressing conflict. Those situations feel emotionally charged and you're likely to worry about the outcome. They also require a great deal of assertiveness, and some people feel flooded by emotion, making it harder for them to articulate their points.

With eating disorders, conflict-avoidance is tied to deeper themes of excessive people-pleasing and of sacrificing your needs. Conflict-avoidance is a powerful form of interpersonal difficulty because it's a complete trap. Conflict is wholly unavoidable. Because conflict is inevitable in your life, you need to cultivate interpersonal effectiveness skills to successfully navigate it.

Your eating disorder, however, likes to keep you stuck trying to avoid conflict at all costs, convincing you that directly addressing the conflict will be the worst thing you can experience. Your eating disorder tells you that if you disagree with someone or argue back, that person might not like you anymore. This is the eating disorder playing to your people-pleasing fears.

When you avoid conflict, several things happen. First, tension is building in the relationship. All relationships have conflict and tension at some point but when they go completely unaddressed, ignored, or are swept under the rug, that tension begins to rot and fester and stink until it becomes resentment. Resentment is much more difficult to repair than momentary conflict. Resentment roots itself firmly and deeply into the relationship's dynamic and, much like gardening, weeding out resentment is hard work.

Part of what contributes to resentment is the other half of what's happening when you avoid conflict; you are sacrificing your needs. When your eating disorder dissuades you from working through conflict with someone, it is tacitly requiring that you relinquish your needs.

Instead of assertively holding to your point or advocating for what you want, your eating disorder positions you to make your needs less important. It will cause you to abandon your point just to get the conflict to end.

As you might imagine, unmet needs are a recipe for resentment. When you feel resentful in your relationship, each individual conflict will feel even more upsetting because now, you're trying to emotionally manage the current, new conflict in addition to the resentment from a history of times where you didn't get your needs met.

This is brilliant work on your eating disorder's part. Your eating disorder hopes you will stay at home with it, a martyr to your unmet needs, using eating disorder behaviors.

Now, your eating disorder has brought you to the point where resentments have built up significantly. When you think of a particular relationship, you get a bitter taste in your mouth or feel a smoldering pang of low-grade anger in your belly. Too many things have gone unsaid, too many needs have gone unmet.

It's hardly possible to feel content with your relationships while sitting on a stack of resentments. Resentment blocks connection and keeps you stuck in the past, your eating disorder bemoaning all the ways this person has wronged you.

As was mentioned earlier, cleaning out resentments is like weeding an overgrown garden. It's difficult, gut-wrenching work requiring unrelenting honesty. When we're truly honest with ourselves, it often hurts. Your eating disorder will continually remind you of this. Remember, it avoids discomfort at all costs. Further, the eating disorder is creating significant interpersonal difficulty by making the relationship overall feel negative to you. You can't hold someone in positive regard when you're secretly angry with them.

Relationships can survive resentment if they're weeded

out. But, as with the overgrown garden, it takes a lot of work to clear away those old emotions. Your eating disorder will discourage you from doing this, opting instead for the familiar misery of leaving things unsaid and feeling unresolved.

It takes courage to confront another person, to ask for something more, and to make yourself vulnerable enough to say you want more from the relationship. Directly addressing and working through resentments and old hurts requires tapping into your wellspring of bravery; it's hidden away somewhere underneath all the lies your eating disorder has told you, convincing you that you can't do it. But, you can.

Sometimes, even after valiant repair attempts, you discover one of your relationships is broken beyond repair. This happens. Sometimes, relationships need to end. Your eating disorder creates interpersonal difficulties by keeping you in relationships you need to get out of.

When a relationship consistently doesn't meet your needs or is harmful to your wellbeing, it's time to consider ending it. Eating disorders use fear of conflict and people-pleasing to keep you in unhealthy relationships long after the point at which you needed to leave. By doing this, your eating disorder ensures you have a constant source of upset in your life, fodder for using eating disorder behaviors.

When your relationships are unhealthy or dissatisfying overall, you are more likely to feel negative about your life as a whole. Our relationships greatly impact our happiness and our outlook on life. When you have several relationships that are hurting you, it's akin to a partly cloudy forecast each day, your life overcast with upset feelings.

In contrast to difficulties in relationships, your eating disorder can cause interpersonal difficulty by isolating you.

Having an eating disorder is an isolating experience. Numerous clients of mine have said over and over that no one understands their eating disorder. And, that's true. It's difficult to understand what it's like to have an eating disorder if you haven't had one yourself.

Because having an eating disorder is such a unique, and oftentimes painful, experience, it is even more important for you to feel connected to and supported by other people. Isolation is ripe with opportunity for feeling down, depressed, hopeless, and lonely. Moreover, when you are alone, you are far more likely to use behaviors. Your eating disorder would like nothing more than for you to retreat from the world, holed up in your home, with only your eating disorder behaviors to comfort you.

Eating disorders disrupt the process of starting new relationships by making you fearful of rejection. It's true. You *could* get rejected. But you could also create a new friendship and the benefit of that far outweighs the risk. Your eating disorder is short-sighted and afraid. It wants for you to think only of the difficulties of starting new relationships to keep you isolated. It wants you all to itself.

It's important for your eating disorder to create interpersonal difficulties for you. To keep you using eating disorder behaviors, your eating disorder will prevent you from stepping out and being brave by making new friends. In your current relationships, your eating disorder wants to trap you in the bind of people-pleasing and not being allowed to work through conflict.

When conflict goes unresolved, minor interpersonal difficulties evolve into a more difficult problem in the form of resentment. Resentment results from unmet needs and unresolved conflict. The cumulative effect of multiple resentment-laden relationships is dissatisfaction with relationships in general. All these circumstances prime the pump for restricting, bingeing, and purging.

Treatment

YOUR EATING DISORDER CAN, and will, try to cause interpersonal difficulties for you in treatment. This is especially true if you are in group therapy of any kind. While in treatment, you're engaged in relationships with your treatment providers. Treatment providers are just people who care deeply but still mess up, say the wrong things, and miscommunicate. Your eating disorder holds treatment providers to the highest standard—an impossible standard in fact—wherein they can't make any mistakes. Try as they might, and as much as they want to achieve it, it's not possible to meet your every need at every moment.

Your eating disorder replicates unhelpful relationship patterns occurring in your external life—with friends, partners, and coworkers—in your relationship with your treatment provider. Your eating disorder causes you to do the same things such as people-please instead of being honest, avoiding conflict or bringing up complaints, and by isolating or disengaging from treatment.

The worst is when your needs have gone unmet in treatment and you're not getting what you want out of therapy but your eating disorder prevents you from bringing this up with your therapist. Instead, you feel secretly, internally frustrated and quit therapy without addressing your concerns. You can see how this pattern keeps the eating disorder going.

If you're involved in any kind of group therapy, your eating disorder will use the same types of patterns to create interpersonal difficulties. Like you and your treatment providers, your fellow group members are only humans who are going to make mistakes, disappoint you, accidentally hurt your feelings on occasion and who're incapable of reading your mind.

The same as in all other relationships, it's important for you to continue to cultivate connections with your peers, to address conflict in the moment to prevent resentments from building up, and to advocate for your own needs.

The Takeaway

INTERPERSONAL DIFFICULTIES ARE some of the most triggering experiences for people with eating disorders. Your eating disorder sets you up by using unhelpful relationship patterns, leaving you in emotional turmoil and priming you to use eating disorder behaviors.

Your eating disorder can create difficulties in your interactions with others when food is involved or force you to resign your needs with food. Your eating disorder maintains unhelpful beliefs within you about relationships—such as claiming that asking for what you need is selfish.

In your relationships, your eating disorder prefers for you to be isolated, to avoid conflict, to let resentment build, and to feel dissatisfied with your relationships overall. Those patterns translate over to your relationships in treatment with both your treatment providers and your peers.

Identifying the interpersonal difficulties your eating disorder creates gives the eating disorder less power and offers you the opportunity to build interpersonal effectiveness skills.

PART IV

Understanding Your Eating Disorder Using ACT

Acceptance and Commitment Therapy

"It's not hard to make decisions when you know what your values are."
-Roy Disney

20

HOW ACT WORKS

Founded by Dr. Steven Hayes, Acceptance and Commitment Therapy, or ACT (pronounced like the verb, *to act*) is another therapeutic modality that emphasizes cognitive (thought) and behavioral (action) change.

In ACT, human suffering is the target of treatment. ACT conceptualizes suffering as being due in large part to our connection to our thoughts, believing them to be true. For example, when you imagine something in your future going horribly wrong and subsequently feel anxious about it, from ACT's perspective the suffering you experience from that is the result of something your mind imagined, not from something happening in the present moment to cause you pain.

ACT's primary goal is to increase "psychological flexibility." This is defined as "the ability to contact the present moment more fully as a conscious human being, and to change or persist in behavior when doing so serves valued ends."[7] Psychological flexibility is when we're able to stay in the present moment, fully aware, behaving and acting in accordance with our values.

ACT increases psychological flexibility through developing six key "processes" or concepts. They are:

1. Cognitive Fusion
2. Acceptance
3. Being Present
4. Self-as-Context
5. Values
6. Committed Action

DON'T WORRY. We're going to go through all these one by one, exploring them within our four categories of Food, Self, Others, and Treatment.

You may have guessed this, and autobiographically know this to be true, but your eating disorder isn't exactly the epitome of psychological flexibility. In fact, it's pretty much as opposed to psychological flexibility as anything could be. Your eating disorder does the opposite of the six processes, such as not allowing you to be present in the moment and preventing you from living life with your true values. We'll examine how this happens with each of the six core processes of ACT.

Problematic Eating Disorder Patterns Explained
Using ACT

21

COGNITIVE FUSION

DEFUSION

Cognitive fusion is the inability to separate yourself from your thoughts. In some ways, this is the thesis of this book—that you are attached to unhelpful patterns resulting from your eating disorder, causing you to mistake who you are with your eating disorder. You become too attached to your eating disorder's thoughts and take them as truths. But, the truth is, that *thoughts are thoughts, not facts.*

One example of cognitive fusion is having the thought, "I'm a loser" and actually believing you are a loser, that that is the truth. However, the truth is you had the *thought* that you were a loser. See the difference? Humans think all kinds of weird, random, bizarre, wild, and even unhelpful thoughts. It's just what human brains do. There's a big difference between having a thought and crawling into bed to cuddle with it.

Your eating disorder knows this. Your eating disorder produces all kinds of thoughts you wouldn't have if you didn't have an eating disorder in the first place. Your eating disorder exploits the principle of cognitive fusion by blurring the lines between what is just a thought and what is the truth.

It wants you to think all the things it whispers in your ear really are true. You're fat. You're a loser. You can't do anything right. No one loves you. You need to lose more weight. Your life, in the end, will resemble a dumpster fire, etc. And so it goes on.

Your eating disorder tries to fuse you to those thoughts because they keep the eating disorder going. As long as you meld with those thoughts, invite them in for dinner, and put them up in your house for the night, they're going to remain permanent fixtures in your mind. It's giving the eating disorder thoughts a room—rent-free—inside your head.

The opposite of cognitive fusion is defusion. ACT aims to decrease cognitive fusion, helping to create psychological distance from your thoughts so those thoughts are not as emotionally charged. When you have some level of detachment from your thoughts, you don't join up with them, automatically believing them. You begin to picture your thoughts maybe as ghosts, little cognitive phantasms floating around in your mind. If you watch them long enough, you'll see one that makes you think, "Yikes, that one's terrifying!"

For me, a horrifying, scary, ghastly thought was: "People will notice your fat rolls. In fact, everyone will. And, they'll run away. No one will ever date you or be friends with you. You're going to die alone, with cats." Terrifying, right? I don't even own a cat. Imagine how damaging it would be if I entertained that thought instead of watching it drift by in my mind, noticing how ghoulish it is. Cognitive fusion isn't about the thought itself. It's about how attached you are to that thought.

The upcoming sections will detail how your eating

disorder uses cognitive fusion to glue you to unhelpful thoughts about the key areas of Food, Yourself, Others, and Treatment, keeping those unhelpful thoughts at the front of your mind, right where they need to be to remain as triggering as possible.

Food

WHEN YOU HAVE AN EATING DISORDER, it tries to fuse you to unhelpful thoughts about food. Your eating disorder wants to fuse you to the most unhelpful thoughts possible, to the cognitively distorted thoughts we talked about earlier in the book. Your eating disorder does this so not only will you have difficult thoughts, but those thoughts will feel like part of you.

Take catastrophizing, for example. An eating disorder thought that exemplifies catastrophizing is: "If I eat more than my daily calorie limit I'm going to gain weight. I'm going to gain weight immediately. I'll never be able to keep my body thin enough. No one will ever want me." Now, the thought itself is an example of catastrophizing. The degree to which you believe it is the cognitive fusion.

If you have this hideous thought, become overwhelmed by it, and spend the rest of your day exploring it and how your life will ultimately resemble a dumpster fire, you're cognitively fused with that thought. If you look at the thought and think, "What a gross, extreme thing to think," then you let it go, you aren't fused with that distortion.

We can also be fused to our thoughts about wanting to use behaviors. Take bingeing as an example. You're bored at home, and boredom is one of your biggest trigger emotions. Not surprisingly, your eating disorder pops up and says, "We should eat something. Actually, there are several packets of microwave popcorn we could eat."

When you're cognitively fused with the thought, you feel like that thought is your only option. You listen to it and proceed to microwave popcorn you didn't even want in the first place. With defusion, you can say to yourself, "I notice I'm having a thought about bingeing," or "I notice my eating disorder is talking right now." You do not immediately join up with the thought, taking its word for it, and doing whatever it says without question.

Perhaps the most insidious, cognitive fusion ninja move your eating disorder pulls is by fusing the eating disorder's thoughts with your own until they've melded together in your concept of your identity. Harkening back to the beginning of the book, it's important to remember that *you are not your eating disorder*. Your eating disorder has its own set of thoughts, usually demoralizing, extreme, unhelpful and unhealthy ones, especially about food, your body, yourself, and your future.

Sometimes, your eating disorder talks a lot. Thought after eating disorder thought pours through your mind. Picture each thought as a leaf floating along on a stream. If you can see it in your mind, imagine that—all of a sudden—a bunch of leaves comes floating down the stream. Maybe there are so many leaves floating along, you can barely see the water beneath.

Guess what? You're the stream. Defusion helps you to recognize that even in times when the eating disorder thoughts rage, there's something more. The leaf and the stream are two separate entities, as are you and your eating disorder.

Self

THROUGH COGNITIVE FUSION, your eating disorder binds you to other unhelpful thoughts about yourself. For eating disorders, the more global and emotionally charged the thought, the better. It's better for your eating disorder if you not only have terrible, miserable, no-good, very bad thoughts about yourself but if you also believe them to be true or to be part of who you are. Some common themes your eating disorder tries to attach you to are as follows:

- Unattractive: According to your eating disorder, you're fat. Or not thin enough. Or not pretty enough. Or too tall or too short or any number of things you could pick apart about yourself. Supported by culture at large, the case for believing you are, in fact, unattractive, can feel compelling at times. That thought can feel true.

When you are cognitively fused, you think, "I *am* fat," and you believe it. With defusion, you say to yourself, "I notice I'm having the thought that I am fat." And, you lovingly let that leaf float on its merry way down the stream.

- Undeserving: Eating disorders seem to love to keep their humans trapped in a weird, sad dungeon of feeling undeserving, wallowing, pleading, wishing to be freed but riddled by the guilt of potential release. Thoughts of being undeserving can look like these: "I can't possibly get this job. Even if I do, it would only be because they couldn't find someone better." Or, "Sure, we're in a relationship now but what if she notices how screwed up I am?" And finally, "No one thinks of me. I'm completely unworthy of anyone's attention."

Your eating disorder uses cognitive fusion to make those thoughts seem true, with a capital T. When you use defusion, you notice the thoughts and let them go. For example, "I notice that I'm having thoughts about being undeserving."

- Unlovable: Thoughts of being unlovable are the holy grail of juicy self-destructiveness ripe with opportunity to drive you into behaviors. Without feeling that you are loveable, why recover?

That's the point your eating disorder will make over and over, harping on you by saying "See, no one remembers you. No one pays attention to you. No one cares. No one loves you." In truth, you are so very loveable. I promise.

When those thoughts come up, say to yourself, "I'm having the thought that I'm unlovable." Then, let that shit go.

As with all the other concepts we've worked through in this book, cognitive fusion sets you up to use behaviors. There's a big difference between telling yourself, "I'm having the thought that I'm a worthless piece of crap right now," and actually believing you are a worthless piece of crap.

When you buy in to the distortions, welcoming them into your mental world, it tacitly gives them validity. Gently remind yourself that the human brain is a marvelous, super-powered miracle organ that sometimes goes off the deep end, generating random, bizarre nonsense. Thoughts are just thoughts, not facts.

Others

Your eating disorder will use cognitive fusion to get you to buddy up with distorted thoughts about other people. Remember, cognitive fusion is not the distorted thought itself but the degree to which you're attached to it. Let go of the thoughts that are not helpful to you and your recovery.

As we go through life engaged in relationships with other people, we inevitably have negative experiences. Unhelpful thoughts spring out of those painful experiences and your eating disorder plans to use cognitive fusion to trap you further, making the original distortion deeper and more difficult to find your way out of.

Anyone who's ever gone through a breakup of a significant relationship knows that on top of the painful feelings of grief or sadness, or sometimes anger and betrayal, our awesome little brains try to make some meaning of the situation. I like to tell people not to draw conclusions during times of emotional crisis.

After breaking up with someone, it's natural that thoughts like, "I can never date again. My heart is fucked up beyond all recognition and I am no good to anyone." There are big implications for believing that thought is true versus noticing, "My thoughts are really extreme right now. I'm even having the thought that I should never date again."

Your eating disorder wants you to take your extreme, post-breakup thoughts and buy into them so you'll restrict, binge, purge, or over-exercise. Worse, when your eating disorder has effectively implemented cognitive fusion, you stop trying with relationships. You quit reaching out, aren't as supported, and don't get to experience the beauty of deep connection.

You can apply those same sorts of thoughts to coworker

relationships and friendships as well. Your eating disorder will generate unhelpful thoughts about your relationships in any domain of your life and then use cognitive fusion to bind you to them. The eating disorder's aim is to prevent you from seeking support and to stop you from feeling connected with other people.

Both supportive relationships and experiencing a deep sense of connection with those you're close to facilitate eating disorder recovery. On the other hand, relationship problems and overall dissatisfaction with your relationships are hugely triggering. Your eating disorder is invested in you buying—wholeheartedly—into its distortions and uses cognitive fusion to entrench you in them.

Treatment

EATING disorders use cognitive fusion profusely when it comes to your thoughts about treatment. We've explored in several chapters of this book the unhelpful, distorted thoughts your eating disorder will produce. With regard to treatment, the eating disorder takes those distortions and glues them to the forefront of your mind. This impairs your ability to focus on treatment, engage, and be present. It's a pretty effective strategy on your eating disorder's part, right? The following sections will discuss how this process can play out.

So, the word on the street is that treatment totally sucks. That's true. Treatment can totally suck. Treatment can be the most miserable, grueling, trying, exhausting, emotionally challenging thing you have to go through. *And*, (remember this from the DBT section?) treatment can also be the most enlightening, restorative, exciting, hopeful, healing thing you ever do for yourself. Both are true. I bet you can guess which kinds of thoughts your eating disorder wants to keep at the front of your mind.

When going through treatment, particularly at a higher level of care, it's completely normal to have thoughts such as, "I'll never get better," or, "Treatment will kill me, I just know it," or, "Treatment won't work for me." But, there's a big difference between having a thought and attaching yourself to that thought, keeping it on your mind all day long.

If we walk this through with an example—say, with the "I'll never get better" thought—we notice that thought is negative, global, and incorrect and stirs up feelings of hopelessness, all of which sound like excellent ammunition for your eating disorder. The eating disorder, again, is setting you up to use behaviors.

You can defuse by creating distance from those thoughts. You can say to yourself, "I notice I'm thinking that treatment won't work for me." Place that thought on a leaf, and let it float downstream in your mind. "I'll never recover," can be changed to, "Right now, I'm thinking that I'll never recover." Notice the thought, then lovingly send it along its way.

I remember a client I worked with who worked very hard in therapy on her recovery. She was doing well but, at one point, went through a significant relapse. Relapse is incredibly common, so much so, you could argue it's inevitable. Following her setback, she felt devastated. I felt for her as she was grappling with feelings of failure, shame, and hopelessness. Her eating disorder used her relapse to trap her, baiting her with all kinds of unhelpful thoughts, primarily telling her she would never recover because she'd had a setback.

Her eating disorder did an excellent job using cognitive fusion. It roped her in until she was certain her situation was hopeless. Because of the cognitive fusion, she stopped attending therapy. After all, according to her eating disorder she was never going to recover, so therapy became pointless. Luckily, she came back to therapy and when we started working together again, we focused on how her eating disorder used cognitive fusion to trigger her, trick her out of going to therapy, and bind her to her hopeless thoughts and feelings.

You see, the eating disorder would prefer it if you spent a whole mess of time wrapped up in that thought, constantly batting it back and forth in your head. "Will I get better? Will I not? Is recovery even possible?" Don't engage with those thoughts. Don't take the bait. Don't get hooked. Once you recognize that it's an unhelpful thought, it's safe to let it go, and carry on with treatment.

The Takeaway

THROUGH COGNITIVE FUSION, your eating disorder can increase the power of cognitive distortions that are already present. Cognitive fusion is not the thought itself but is how tied you feel to it, how true you believe it to be.

Your eating disorder uses cognitive fusion to make it seem harder to escape unhelpful, triggering thoughts about food, yourself, other people, and treatment. ACT helps people to defuse from their thoughts, taking a mindful perspective, noticing that thoughts are just thoughts, not necessarily truths.

22

EXPERIENTIAL AVOIDANCE
ACCEPTANCE

Experiential avoidance, as it sounds, is when you avoid rather than allow yourself to experience something. Experiential avoidance is often talked about in the context of emotions, specifically how most people tend to avoid uncomfortable emotions.

Experiential avoidance is the opposite of acceptance. For example, perhaps you hate feeling the emotion of sadness. You refuse to allow yourself to feel any sadness (avoiding experiencing this emotion) rather than accepting that you feel sad, opening yourself up to it, feeling it, and moving on. ACT aims to decrease experiential avoidance and increase acceptance.

Acceptance is an interesting concept because it requires that we open ourselves to uncomfortable feelings and experiences without defense, without resisting them. Acceptance doesn't mean you like the upset emotion you're having. It does not mean you condone how someone in your life is acting. It does not mean that if you had the power to, you wouldn't change things. It simply means you acknowledge that things are as they are and that you are willing to deal with them in their current state.

Eating disorders do not allow for acceptance. Your eating disorder prefers to get you caught up in struggle. Your eating disorder wants you to fight your feelings. It wants you to resist change. It wants you to be perfectionistic and rigid instead of flexible and accepting.

Your eating disorder uses experiential avoidance in several ways. First, it may involve experiential avoidance by avoiding foods themselves. Second, your eating disorder wants you to avoid your feelings at all costs because, by allowing yourself to work through your feelings, you will ultimately discover the underlying causes of your eating disorder. And, that's not good news for your eating disorder. Lastly, your eating disorder will use experiential avoidance in your social life and in treatment. When it does this, your eating disorder tricks you out of trying new things, growing, and becoming stronger and braver in the process.

Food

PART of what makes experiential avoidance so effective is that it builds up the struggle in your mind, making it out to be worse than it really is. Now, don't get me wrong, sometimes you think something's going to be awful and it turns out you're correct. However, your eating disorder wants to make *everything* seem much worse than it will be.

You know that saying, "psyching yourself out"? That's what your eating disorder is doing. In your mind, it's making things out to seem much worse than they might be to keep you stuck and to continue to make you use behaviors.

We can easily see how experiential avoidance happens

with food. When your eating disorder has you stuck in a pattern of restricting, the foods you're "not allowed" to eat, you avoid. Once in recovery, part of the work is adding these foods back into your diet and repairing your relationship with them.

I remember a client I had who restricted pasta because her eating disorder forbade her from eating it. Pasta had become evil. As she worked in recovery to re-introduce this food, she bumped up against experiential avoidance. For several weeks, she talked with me in therapy and with her dietitian about how she could not eat pasta. It would be "the worst thing ever." She would "feel fat" after eating it. And, her "body wouldn't do well with it."

After several sessions of directly working on experiential avoidance, she accepted the challenge of eating her fear food, pasta. When she actually sat down to eat it, it was difficult. She felt anxious beforehand. During her attempt to eat it, she enjoyed the taste of the noodles. Afterward, she experienced feelings of guilt brought on by her eating disorder shaming her for breaking its rules. But, she had come to a place of acceptance.

She was willing to experience anxiety and guilt momentarily to get her closer to her goal of recovery. She accepted that, for her, having a healthy relationship with food and her body meant she had to trust it when she ate pasta. She accepted that the first few times of eating this fear food would again be difficult. And, even though it *was* difficult at first, she accepted the challenge. Now, she enjoys a greater variety of food, including pasta and other delicious foods previously banned by her eating disorder.

Experiential avoidance is easy to see when it comes to restricting food but you can also see it with bingeing and purging. There, the eating disorder uses experiential avoidance to get you to give in to the behaviors, rather than waiting and wading through the anxiety of when you're triggered to binge or purge.

With bingeing, I work with people to increase mindfulness to a point where they're able to recognize when they're going to binge. Many people binge automatically and often don't realize they're bingeing until they're mid-binge or after they're done bingeing completely. Once someone has used mindfulness enough, they become aware of their actions during the bingeing process.

You can recognize when you're in the kitchen standing in front of the pantry with a bunch of foods laid out in front of you. You know what your eating disorder is trying to get you to do. Once you have awareness, you begin practicing what choices you'd like to make. In this case, the choice is to start a binge or stop bingeing after you've begun.

Stopping a binge in the middle or resisting a binge from the get-go is rough! It's miserable and hard and awful and terrible, and maybe you feel like you will die from the feelings that come up when you choose a path other than using behaviors. But, I promise you, you won't.

Your eating disorder manipulates you with experiential avoidance, convincing you that choosing behaviors is better than experiencing the tough feelings from *not* using behaviors. In the moment, maybe behaviors do feel better, easier. Overall, however, they're causing you more pain by keeping you stuck in an eating disorder. The challenge is to accept that you're going to feel really crappy for a few minutes now because this will help you to feel recovered later.

The same concept applies to purging. When people feel triggered to purge, they usually report an overwhelming desire to follow through. My clients have told me they feel so anxious they could crawl out of their skin if they didn't purge. Once they purge, the anxiety goes away.

By purging, the behavior is reinforced because it *temporarily* alleviated the anxiety. Your eating disorder will use experiential avoidance to convince you that you can't ride out the feelings that come up when you want to purge. Your eating disorder refuses to allow you to feel incredibly uncomfortable in the short-term, so instead, you'll avoid these feelings and purge anyway.

Your eating disorder uses experiential avoidance to directly interfere with you repairing your relationship with food. Experiential avoidance also perpetuates eating disorder behaviors by making you use behaviors rather than accept difficult, temporary emotions inevitable in the recovery process.

Self

MIXED in with uncomfortable feelings about food are usually difficult feelings about yourself. Your eating disorder uses experiential avoidance to get you to avoid any tough feelings you have about yourself, even feelings unrelated to food. Experiential avoidance creates a vicious cycle wherein you avoid painful feelings, use behaviors more, then feel a greater amount of difficult emotions from using those very behaviors.

The following is something one of my former clients wrote about how her eating disorder uses experiential avoidance:

My eating disorder is all about avoiding feelings I'm afraid to face. Initially, it was a way to avoid feeling inadequate. I wanted to measure up to my boyfriend's high standards, and I wanted to feel just as self-controlled as my other girlfriends. Eventually, however, it became so much of a habit—a way of life—that breaking away from the eating disorder rules meant facing a feeling I really couldn't bear...guilt. The guilt and regret and worthlessness I felt from eating what I considered to be unsafe or too much was excruciating. I had to continue my eating disorder to avoid those feelings. When my eating disorder was at its worst, my behaviors protected me from much more than guilt, however, they numbed me from feeling anything at all. I didn't feel pleasure, sure, but I didn't have to feel pain either. Breaking away from my ED meant introducing a whole new world of emotions.

This excerpt illustrates the vicious cycle in action. First, this client had felt inadequate, a very tough emotion to feel toward yourself and, unfortunately, not an uncommon feeling either. Then, the eating disorder interjected by having her use behaviors rather than doing the difficult, worthwhile work of confronting the feelings of inadequacy. After continuing to use behaviors, the inadequacy continued, guilt was layered on by the eating disorder and her feelings of pleasure were dampened.

Another client wrote this about experiential avoidance:

Sadness, rejection, loneliness, and frustration, to name a few, are feelings that often arise, which result in eating disorder behaviors. Whether it's not eating as a way to take control or bingeing to numb the feelings, escaping to the eating disorder brings a momentary false reality that distances me from my feelings, providing a glimpse of ease during painful times. This extends beyond the specific behaviors and I get caught up in a new problem the eating disorder created (through eating or not eating) which allows me to focus on the ED instead of the reality, the reality that includes my emotions.

This passage highlights several key points. First, experiential avoidance occurs with the avoidance of emotions. Of course, sadness, rejection, loneliness, and frustration are tough feelings to sit with. The challenge is to accept (not to like) that in that moment, you're feeling sad or rejected or lonely or frustrated.

When your eating disorder makes you completely unwilling to experience painful emotions, even though those emotions are temporary, you will use behaviors. Another point my client makes is that the solution of avoiding your feelings and using behaviors doesn't really resolve anything. In fact, it creates more problems. The first excerpt spoke to the same point.

Lastly, one of the most powerful points the excerpt made, is that reality includes difficult, uncomfortable, painful emotions. They're part of life as a human being. When you avoid uncomfortable emotions, you avoid getting to know yourself. You avoid significant parts of who you are. You avoid the markers you need to pay attention to, in order to grow. When your eating disorder causes you to avoid your experiences, it stunts your growth and prevents your potential from turning into your actual.

Difficult emotions cannot be avoided forever. By avoiding your experience of them and using eating disorder behaviors instead, the vicious cycle of eating disorder behaviors continues.

Others

YOUR EATING DISORDER uses experiential avoidance in your relationships with other people as well. Earlier in the book, we talked about people-pleasing and avoiding conflict. Both these can certainly be considered experiential avoidance. Eating disorders like to build things up in your mind to seem much worse than they are likely to be. This includes confrontation. However, as we explored earlier in the book, confrontation is necessary at times. Given that people cannot know your every want and need, you'll have to bring things up on your own including complaints and constructive criticism.

Eating disorders use experiential avoidance of conflict to keep you stuck in situations that aren't working, resulting in continued frustration and upset. Both of those feelings are powerful triggers for using eating disorder behaviors.

Your eating disorder can use experiential avoidance in another, more insidious, way. Your eating disorder will use experiential avoidance to limit your ability to be vulnerable. Aside from the fact that eating disorders generally interfere significantly with people's social lives—because they directly affect food, making all social activities involving food decidedly unpleasant and arduous—eating disorders also like to block you from feeling deeply connected to, or supported by other people.

To build connection, we must be vulnerable. Connection requires that we show up as our true, authentic selves, not as another version of ourselves showing only the parts we think others will like or trying to highlight parts of who we are to impress them. If you want real relationships, there's no way to sidestep vulnerability. If you want real recovery, there's no way to sidestep vulnerability either. The catch is that vulnerability feels, well, vulnerable.

My clients have described it to me as feeling like they

might throw up, feeling scared, and anxious. I can relate to those feelings myself. Lots of situations require us to be vulnerable. Waiting to hear back from someone you're hoping to have another date with—Vulnerable. Meeting someone new and hoping you can become friends—Vulnerable. Stepping into a new leadership role at work —vulnerable.

But because vulnerability tends to feel intense to most people, and because being vulnerable often has a great payoff, your eating disorder wants you to avoid that experience. Your eating disorder has no acceptance of the necessity of vulnerability.

Instead, what your eating disorder will do is disempower you by scaring you about vulnerability. Your eating disorder will tell you vulnerability is too risky, that it's not worth moving through the fear, and that you'll get rejected or fail and obviously never live through it. Even worse, your eating disorder will block you from vulnerability by telling you that you're undeserving of the joy that could come from taking a risk.

Sometimes, experiential avoidance manifests in the form of isolation. Eating disorders are known to keep people at home alone, avoiding food and fun, left with only the disorder itself for comfort. Reaching out to others can be intimidating. It's hard to build new friendships, to maintain established ones, and not easy to work through the inevitable conflict authentic relationships entail. But, you *can* do it.

Rather than fighting the experience of vulnerability, connection, and joy as your eating disorder would have you do, make room in your head and heart to accept the tougher parts that always come along with meaningful, real relationships.[8]

Treatment

YOU CAN PROBABLY IMAGINE that experiential avoidance takes place with regard to treatment. Of course, your eating disorder isn't going to be a fan of treatment as this directly contradicts its mission of keeping itself going. However, it's helpful to understand some specific ways in which your eating disorder will interfere with treatment.

Your eating disorder may prevent you from seeking treatment in the first place, delaying the process by causing you to procrastinate. We'll talk about this in an upcoming chapter on "inaction" rather than in this chapter on experiential avoidance. Instead, we'll explore how experiential avoidance takes place once you've already begun treatment.

When we review our definition of experiential avoidance, we know experiential avoidance happens when you avoid something rather than allowing yourself to experience it. The crux of experiential avoidance is avoiding painful emotions. And, confronting painful emotions lies at the heart of the recovery process. All those feelings that gave rise to your eating disorder in the first place, that your eating disorder once helped you survive, now need to be brought to light with gentleness, compassion, and support from a kickass treatment team.

Your eating disorder wants you to avoid difficult feelings and difficult work in therapy. Sometimes in therapy, people leave out important things they need to talk about because they feel too painful to confront. However, those are usually the things needing the most attention, love, and care.

Your eating disorder wants you to focus on how awful it could feel to confront your feelings of inadequacy, rather than how healing it will be. Your eating disorder wants you to avoid working on family dynamics that make recovery difficult rather than working through times of trial as a family, as a team. Your eating disorder definitely doesn't want you to confront the problem of identity, when you have to get brave enough to figure out who you are without your eating disorder.

The antidote to experiential avoidance is acceptance. When you choose acceptance, you're not skipping around the room gleefully in blithe disregard of your painful emotions. No, acceptance doesn't mean you're overjoyed about the trauma you've endured and what it will mean to work through it as you recover, or that you've forgotten how people have treated you or that you'll tolerate poor treatment in the future.

Rather, acceptance is a strong, empowered, mature stance where you agree that in order to create a recovered life for yourself, you're willing to let feelings wash over you and to look at them honestly, even when you're afraid. You acknowledge that you're willing to get temporarily uncomfortable, to ultimately experience a greater sense of peace.

The Takeaway

YOUR EATING DISORDER hinges on experiential avoidance. With experiential avoidance, your eating disorder convinces you that trying to gloss over feelings, stuff them, ignore them, deny them is in your best interest. In reality, it's only in your eating disorder's best interest.

Your eating disorder makes you fearful and unwilling to take on challenges with food, to confront uncomfortable feelings toward yourself, to work through difficult times with others, and to shrink away from treatment. With acceptance, you can open yourself to feeling difficult emotions, knowing that even if you don't like what you're going through, you can get through it and, if you're willing, you can learn from it.

23

STUCK IN THE PAST, TRAPPED IN THE FUTURE

BEING PRESENT

Being stuck in the past or fearfully trapped in your future is the opposite of being mindful and present in the current moment. It is as it sounds. It happens when you spend more of your time thinking and feeling about the past or the future than you do about *the now*.

ACT encourages individuals to be present in the current moment, taking a non-judgmental, observing stance to what is happening around you and within you. In ACT, being present increases psychological flexibility. The overarching goal of ACT is to increase psychological flexibility.

When you are not present in the current moment, you've either slipped into the past or stepped forward into the future. It's natural to wonder about your future or review what happened in the past. Your eating disorder, however, takes this to an extreme, getting you stuck in worry about the future or mired in past regrets. When your eating disorder puts its blinders on, focusing in on your worries about the future or painful things from your past, you feel upset. Specifically, you are apt to feel hopeless, shameful, and discouraged, all of which are highly triggering emotions.

Another reason why your eating disorder wants to get you stuck in the future or trapped in the past is because it decreases your likelihood to take action *now*. When you obsess over what might happen or beat yourself up for whatever has already occurred, your focus, energy, and efforts are not vested in the present, including what you presently need to do to create recovery.

Getting stuck in the past or trapped in the future keeps the vicious cycle of the eating disorder going. One of my clients wrote this about her eating disorder pulling her away from the present moment:

> *After dealing with anorexia for years, I began bingeing and over-exercising. I ruminated over the body I used to have. This would translate into fear and panic about losing weight and being worthy or good enough to experience what other people do in a lifetime.*

Here, you can see her eating disorder has her cornered. Her eating disorder makes her feel crappy about what her body was like in the past while it simultaneously scares her about her future.

Stuck in the past, trapped in the future is a brilliant strategy if you're an eating disorder. With the past, there often isn't anything you can do to change things. It's already happened. With the future, you have no way of knowing what will happen, so instead of believing things will go well, your eating disorder likes you to "what if" yourself into oblivion, ramping up your anxiety and maximizing how much it can trigger you.

The following sections will examine in detail how your

eating disorder gets you stuck in the past and trapped in the future with regard to food, yourself, other people, and treatment.

Food

FOOD PROVIDES endless opportunities to get stuck in the past or worry about the future. When you have an eating disorder, the rigid food rules you have to live by provide an opportunity to criticize yourself for what you previously ate. I can't tell you how many times clients have told me that they ate something that violated their eating disorder's rules and became absolutely stuck on it.

Clients have told me that they've thought about "breaking the rules" for days. They walk around thinking through what they ate, stressing about how "unhealthy" it was, and counting the calories they ate. Similarly, when clients binge, their eating disorders can get them stuck on the binge, regretting it and mentally beating themselves up about it for days.

When it comes to what you already ate, what's done is done. Once you've eaten, all you can do is move forward and make choices that support your recovery. Your eating disorder wants for you to ruminate and obsess over past food choices so you can beat yourself up. When you shame yourself for "messing up," you are triggered to use more behaviors.

Further, the more you dwell on the past, seeing things through your eating disorder's perspective, the more hopeless you'll feel about your future. Your eating disorder wants to discourage you about your future and your potential to recover so it can have you all to itself.

Looking in the other direction, your eating disorder likes to trap you in worries about your future with food. One of the ways your eating disorder disconnects you from the present moment is through food planning. It's normal to think about what you might like for dinner, what you need to purchase at the grocery store, and what meals you could make ahead for the week. Your eating disorder takes this normal process and twists it to its own advantage to suit its agenda.

Getting trapped in an anxious food future can look like counting and strategizing down to every calorie. Clients I've worked with have tracked every calorie they ate and strategized about what they would do with every future calorie. In the throes of my own eating disorder, I planned every meal down to every calorie for an entire week. My elaborate tally system, check-box- ridden, was a perfectionistic prison.

My eating disorder did this to create massive amounts of anxiety. Think about it, how can anyone realistically comply with a food plan calculated to the calorie? There's no flexibility, no room for spontaneity, no space for change—and there definitely isn't any joy.

If you find yourself reading endless recipes looking for the perfect one or making charts to track your food intake, or using apps on your phone to assess your progress, your eating disorder has pulled you away from the present moment. Anxiety about breaking the rules is keeping you in an imagined, uncertain, what-if hell.

The same concepts apply to bingeing and purging. If you're spending time planning how to sneak away during your lunch at work to buy binge foods and secretly purge before your break is over, your eating disorder is preventing you from living in the moment. Obsessing over the next time you get to use behaviors is one of the ways your eating disorder keeps you in the future and in its grasp.

Given that you'll need to eat multiple meals and snacks per day, your eating disorder happily takes advantage of the numerous opportunities to stir you up about what's already happened and what *might* happen.

Self

Your eating disorder will keep you stuck in the past about things you've already done. It will also scare you about aspects of your future that haven't come to pass. As with food, your eating disorder does this to cause you to feel upset. Feeling regret and shame about the past and feeling anxiety and fear about the future can be incredibly triggering. Getting you stuck in the past or fixated on the future also distracts you from focusing on your current growth or work with yourself, limiting your personal development and distracting you from recovery.

When it comes to looking back into your past, your eating disorder tends to focus on two areas. First, it will review things you've done, producing feelings of guilt, shame, and regret. Second, it will focus more broadly on who you used to be, manipulating aspects of your identity at a past time in your life to make you feel bad about how you were. Both these strategies disconnect you from your present self. When you connect with yourself in the present moment, you can appreciate your current strengths and you are able to recognize areas you want to improve.

The first way your eating disorder gets you stuck in the past is by ruminating on things that have happened in the past or decisions you've already made. Looking back at what we've done is important. We can learn a lot with healthy retrospection. It can give insight into your motivation, informing you about how you grow, and give you direction about how to move forward. Healthy retrospection is necessary for personal growth.

This is not what your eating disorder is doing. Your eating disorder is wallowing in regret and bathing you in shame about things you can't change. For example, let's say you had an opportunity to take a promotion at your job but you decided not to. At the time, you had good reasons for politely turning it down. Maybe the job had terrible hours despite excellent pay? Maybe you weren't ready to move up in the company or wanted more time to develop in your current role? Those all sound like completely understandable reasons for passing up a promotion.

Now you're thinking about what the next phase in your career will look like. Healthy retrospection is when you look back with gentleness, compassion, and objectivity to learn from that experience so you can plan for the next move you'll make.

What your eating disorder does is not healthy retrospection; it just buries you in regret. What if you'd taken that promotion? Where would you be now? How entitled were you to pass that up? What if not taking that previous promotion has hampered your chances of ever moving up again? *You idiot.*

When you dwell in the past, reviewing your decisions over and over again with a critical eye, you're unable to focus on what you need to do *now*. Moreover, your eating disorder is likely to make you feel bad about something you don't need to feel bad about. In this case, your eating disorder is trying to make you regret a justifiable decision, not to mention that sometimes we make mistakes, legitimate mistakes that were harmful to ourselves or others. Though this isn't pleasant, it's normal—and unavoidable.

Your eating disorder wants to layer on the shame about past mistakes. When it does this, the feeling of shame is so overwhelming you can't examine objectively what you need to do to move on and learn from it. It does no one, including yourself, any good to stay stuck on your perceived failures.

In a bigger sense, eating disorders like to make you beat yourself up for who you used to be, making you think back to an earlier version of yourself: your college self, your high school self, your middle school self. Looking back, though, anyone could shame themselves to death about the things they did that they'd now consider dumb, or about embarrassing moments they had, or people they hurt.

And, that's exactly what your eating disorder is going to do. It is going to suffocate you with shame about who you were in the past, who you were as a normal part of development. Everyone can look back and think, "I wish I would have known this," or, "I wish I hadn't done that," because learning through making mistakes is inevitable and necessary for growth.

Your eating disorder blows the missteps out of proportion. Instead of allowing for guilt, it brings about shame. With guilt, we look back at our behavior and feel a twinge of pain when those actions were out of line with our values. We learn, make amends, and move on trying to live out our values the best way we can. When your eating disorder uses shame, it makes you look back and think, "I am bad" instead of noticing what you did wasn't in line with who you want to be. Shame breeds rumination and ultimately leads to behaviors.

In contrast to your eating disorder fixating on your past mistakes, it can also get you unnecessarily worked up about your future. As with dwelling in the past, getting stuck in the future prevents you from connecting with your current strengths and present areas for improvement, both of which get in the way of recovery.

When you look at your future through your eating disorder's perspective, you are overcome with uncertainty, anxiety, and fear. Your eating disorder's assumption about your future is that bad things will happen.

Eating disorders like to "what if" you mercilessly. The what-if game is a great strategy for it to employ. First, it takes up a ton of time and mental energy to play the game. Second, there's no way prove what will happen, which produces a great deal of anxiety. And, your eating disorder then uses this anxiety to immobilize you. It's hard to work on yourself when you're focused on every potential catastrophic outcome.

The examples I've heard from clients are endless. "What if I never find someone to be with?" "What if I never get married?" "What if I can't find a job?" "What if I never get to have children?" And, of course, there's the ultimate eating disorder what-if: "What if I gain weight?" All these anxiety-laden thoughts bring your focus away from the present.

If you want to be in a relationship, great! In the present, you can work on yourself, think about what you want in a partner, learn how to be a good partner, and take on the challenge of meeting people. Want a new job? Fantastic! Right now, you can look at what you need to do to prepare for interviews, what kind of career you want, and what values you want in the company you work for.

By building up anxiety and worry about your future, your eating disorder distracts you from improving in the now. This is because any personal development in the present will threaten the eating disorder's existence.

Looking backward into the past or forward into an unpredictable future provides endless opportunity for your eating disorder to upset you, trigger you, and distract you from learning, improving, and appreciating yourself *now*.

Others

EATING disorders can easily get you stuck in thinking about past relationships and scare you unnecessarily about future ones. Relationships are incredibly meaningful to us humans, which is why your eating disorder likes shrouding them in regret and clouding your future hopes with anxiety.

People who have eating disorders tend to be extremely loving, caring, kind, considerate individuals with strong intuitions, who are usually quite skilled at reading others. This makes them wonderful friends, partners, co-workers, and family members. It's only because you have these positive traits in the first place, that your eating disorder can take all this strength and weaponize it, causing you to get stuck in the past or stress about the future of your relationships.

I once worked with a client whose ex-boyfriend was extremely unkind to her. In fact, he was emotionally and verbally abusive, constantly putting her down. One of his favorite things to criticize her about was her appearance. In his eyes, she was never "in shape" enough. Her breasts were too small. She was never pretty enough or dressed up enough to impress him. And although the relationship had ended long ago, my client's eating disorder entangled itself in the abusive messages she received from this past relationship.

When she spoke from her eating disorder's perspective,

it sounded a whole lot like her ex. Her eating disorder ruminated, reviewing over and over how—if she could have just been thinner, prettier, whatever-er—he wouldn't have left. Her eating disorder manipulated her into believing the abusive messages he'd given and simultaneously trapped her in the past by focusing on how she'd failed in his eyes.

This happens when abuse isn't involved as well. Your eating disorder will take any past regret from any of your relationships and make it the focus of your attention, rather than what you need to focus on in the present moment.

For instance, say you had a big argument with your friend a few weeks ago. You both said hurtful things but talked through them and apologized to each other. Your friend told you everything was okay. But, your eating disorder doesn't want you to be okay. It wants you to beat yourself up over the things you've already worked through.

If you dwell on what happened, you can shame yourself. You can also feel unnecessary fear that the relationship has been damaged—despite your friend's assurance that it hasn't—decreasing your sense of closeness with her and making you less likely to seek her support. It's a giant setup.

The future of relationships is scary even if you don't have an eating disorder. It can be scary to think about people leaving our lives and people rejecting us, about not living up to others' expectations or about our loved ones dying. Your eating disorder loves to trap you in the future with *what ifs*. What if he breaks up with you? What if you can't keep your friendship? What if your parents divorce? It never ends. The potential for anxiety is endless as well. The eating disorder keeps you fearful, anxious, and stressed about future scenarios, many of which may never actually happen.

Aside from creating problems with your relationships in

your mind that may not happen, the eating disorder keeps you trapped in future anxieties to disempower you. Your eating disorder wants you to only think of the worst possible outcomes of what could happen in the future, and doesn't want you to believe that if something bad did happen, you'd be able to work through it. The anxiety you experience from potential future worries is heightened by your inability to completely control the future especially when other people are involved.

Staying stuck in the past or trapped in the future means your eating disorder is trying to emotionally dysregulate you, to trigger you to use behaviors. When you're present in the now, you can fully connect with others and you can collaboratively work through disagreements. Your eating disorder is invested in causing chaos in your relationships to fuel your restricting, bingeing, and purging.

Treatment

EATING disorders keep you stuck in the past and trapped in the future about treatment. Your eating disorder can take several different approaches to burying you in the past. One way eating disorders do this is by overwhelming you about how bad the eating disorder itself is. Ironic, I know.

Your eating disorder will review with you how severe your eating disorder is, noting things and shaming you for every time you use behaviors. It will convince you your eating disorder is so horrible you could never recover. Its aim is to make you feel hopeless and dissuade you from pursuing recovery.

Another way eating disorders entangle you in the past is by reminding you of those times in the past when treatment hasn't worked out for you. But seeking treatment several times is actually quite common and normal; many people with eating disorders seek multiple rounds of treatment, even at a higher level of care.

I once had a client who had been to residential treatment three times but who needed to go back because her behaviors had become severe again, despite all her efforts. She recounted to me, crying, all her past experiences at higher level of care. She explained she had "already failed" and that nothing had ever helped her in the past, so she didn't believe anything could help her in the future.

Ultimately, with the support of her family, she returned to residential. There, she made great strides in recovery and returned to outpatient therapy with a new energy and a whole lot of progress under her belt.

When your eating disorder dwells on past treatment, it's because it doesn't want you moving forward in your present treatment. Eating disorders do this when they are scared because few emotions are more immobilizing than hopelessness.

Speaking of immobilizing, terrifying you about future treatment is one way your eating disorder sabotages your recovery. Your eating disorder will create great anxiety, even dread, about whether or not treatment will work. In addition to anticipating all the ways treatment will suck and be horrible and ruin your life, your eating disorder likes to engage in *what-if*-ing your overall recovery. What if you don't recover? What if you don't do well enough in treatment? What if you can't stop using behaviors? What if you have to go back to higher level of care again?

What if? What if? What if?

What-if-ing is a distraction. If your mind is off in the future, wandering around alone and terrified, you're not likely to take steps you need to recover in the now. Excessively worrying about the future pulls you out of the present moment and keeps you away from doing the hard yet worthwhile work of recovery you need to do now.

The Takeaway

BEING STUCK in the past and trapped in the future is the opposite of being fully present in the now. Your eating disorder heaps on shame and regret about things that happened in the past with food, with behaviors, with decisions, in relationships, and even in past levels of treatment. The more shameful and stuck you are in the past, the less hope you have for the future and, the more likely you are to be triggered.

Likewise, your eating disorder traps you in the future, conjuring up all possible bad outcomes with food, behaviors, relationships, and treatment. The anxiety of the unknown immobilizes you, distracting you from the progress you can make *right now*. Reconnecting with the now empowers you to focus your efforts on recovery, appreciate your strengths, and show up authentically to be present with the other people in your life.

24

LOSS OF PERSPECTIVE

SELF-AS-CONTEXT

One of the six core concepts of ACT is called Self-As-Context. Self-as-context can be a little confusing to understand. For our purposes, we'll define self-as-context as the observing self, the part of you that can observe your thoughts and feelings from a distance. The observing self is the part of you that makes defusion (detaching from your thoughts) possible.

With self-as-context, you're able to zoom out and take a big-picture perspective about your experiences. One metaphor used in ACT to help us better understand the observing self is to think of life as a play happening on stage and yourself as the director, watching it from a distance rather than being one of the actors. We'll explore this in detail with examples to make this concept clear.

As with all the other concepts we've discussed, your eating disorder will twist it to serve its own purposes. Self-as-context is an extremely helpful skill to develop. When you're able to see yourself from the observing self perspective, you can defuse from unhelpful thoughts and accept difficult emotions. When you have an eating disorder, it completely prevents you from seeing things from the self-as-context perspective. It only allows you to see things through its own warped eating disorder lens.

The opposite of self-as-context is what I refer to as *confusing your self with your context* (thinking you are an actor in the play but really your perspective is that of the director). Confusing self and context means you are unable to see that you are the one who can observe your thoughts, who can step back and take a big-picture, transcendent view of your self and your life.

You are mired in your singular view of your life. When you can see yourself in context, from the observing self-perspective, you can get out of your head and observe yourself objectively.

Let's examine how this transpires in our four categories of Food, Self, Others, and Treatment.

Food

IT MIGHT BE HELPFUL to use a metaphor for self-as-context or the observing self, throughout these sections. Let's say that your life is a TV episode. There are things happening during the episode. There are people in the episode you're watching. And, you're one of the characters too.

Self-as-context is when you feel like you aren't in the show but that you're actually watching an episode of your own life, from an outsider's perspective.

What's neat about this is that the observing self perspective is inherently more detached from what's going on, including from being entangled in difficult thoughts, feelings, and behaviors. Let's use our observing self with food and explore how your eating disorder gets in the way.

As an example, you decide to attend a holiday party for work. When you arrive, there's a whole table full of food that your eating disorder has outlawed. You know your eating disorder will freak out, making you feel anxious and guilty if you eat those foods. But, you also want to be able to enjoy those foods and the party without feeling terrible before, during, and after.

When you look at this situation from only the eating disorder's perspective, all you can see is the potential disaster from eating the foods at the party. You can feel the anxiety and fear. And, you can anticipate the guilt that will follow if you partake in the holiday offerings. Your eating disorder does not allow you to see things from the part of you called your observing self. It does not allow for self-as-context.

With self-as-context, the situation would look like this: You walk into the room and notice the table full of items your eating disorder forbids you from eating. At this point, you decide to connect with a wise part of yourself—with your observing self. In your mind, you picture yourself step-ping out of your body, watching yourself as a character on this TV episode. You imagine the episode playing out. You can even narrate it in your mind: "Today in this episode in Food, [insert your name here] goes to the holiday party."

In the holiday party episode of your food life, you watch yourself walking over to the table and see yourself looking over the foods there. You see yourself smelling them, noticing which ones entice you and which ones don't. You see how you pause for a moment to check in with how hungry or full you are and to inquire as to what your body is asking for.

With this information, you watch yourself on this episode choose the foods you want. You watch as you eat each food mindfully, appreciating and savoring the foods. And, finally, you watch the episode conclude when you stop eating after you feel your fullness, listening to your body's limits.

Using self-as-context can help you to get the big picture perspective on situations that could normally feel overwhelming. With the help of your observing self, you can look back on the holiday party and say to yourself, "Good episode!"

Self

LET'S WATCH ANOTHER EPISODE. This one is called "[insert your name here] goes shopping for new clothes." Your eating disorder will make you feel self-conscious or critical toward your body, if not downright shameful about it.

When you have an eating disorder, you see your body through its perspective. You see everything it thinks is flawed and focus on everything it would have you change until you can't feel anything other than deep dissatisfaction. When you can't use self-as-context and you're left with only your eating disorder's point of view on your body, you're set up to use eating disorder behaviors.

The episode begins. You walk into the store and see a variety of t-shirts folded on a table. You wander over and notice you like a couple of the designs. You want to try some of them on so you pick up a couple of shirts and walk back to the fitting room. Under the harsh, fluorescent lights, you see one of the shirts is extremely unflattering; the material and color don't look good on you, and the shirt just doesn't fit quite right.

From your eating disorder's point of view, you see your

body, not the shirt, as the problem. Your eating disorder begins to criticize you, telling you you're fat. It tells you your stomach and your arms are hideous. It tells you that the shirt would look better if you were thinner. You feel anxious followed by a warm flush of shame. You agree with your eating disorder. You *are* hideous. You feel as though you could cry.

When you use your observing self, you can watch the episode play out, even if it's a crappy episode. So, let's say this is a rough episode where things don't go as you'd like them to. You find the shirts you like and take them back to the dressing room to try them on. Much to your dismay, one of the shirts does not do your beauty justice.

Using the observing self, you step outside yourself, noticing what is happening, watching your life as though it's an episode. You see the main character, you, looking sad in a dressing room. You watch yourself tear up as your eating disorder says vicious things to you.

Using self-as-context, you can see this is a sad episode, rather than feeling that the eating disorder is correct. In review, you look back and say, "That episode sucked. The protagonist wound up feeling terrible over a t-shirt. Hope the next episode is better."

Self-as-context and the observing self are important because they offer an alternative point of view that is wholly different from that of the eating disorder. Self-as-context is grounded in reality, is objective. It enables you to detach from difficult feelings your eating disorder is making you feel toward yourself.

Others

I BET you've had lots of interesting episodes with other people. I know I have. I've had episodes that warmed my heart because someone was so supportive, other episodes where I thought to myself, "That's not how I saw things going," and heartbreaking episodes where things didn't work out with someone I loved. And, I've had episodes I can only describe as highly dysfunctional. Let's do one of those episodes.

Imagine a group of people in your life, say your family or coworkers or a group of your friends, can be a little dysfunctional. Now, this is all hypothetical and it's just you and me talking so have some fun with it.

In this episode of your life, [insert your name] goes to dinner with [insert names of supporting characters]. Picture it however you need to. If you want, you can draw some inspiration from dysfunctional dinners you've had in the past. Don't worry, we'll put that disclaimer at the beginning of the episode that says, "This episode is fictional and is not based on any person or event."

Set the scene. I'm going to use a group of friends as an example. Your awesome best friend is there with you at the dinner table, alongside another friend you don't know very well. The few times you've interacted with her, she's come across as somewhat self-conscious and sweet. Then, there's your best friend's friend. You know, she's the one you probably wouldn't choose to hang out with if she wasn't involved in your best friend's life. She's can be a bit harsh, loud, sometimes curt.

And here's the scene. Everyone's seated at the dinner table in a trendy restaurant. You're really only there because you want to hang with your best friend; you don't mind the second woman, but the final woman in the group really rubs you the wrong way. You're feeling triggered because you're unfamiliar with the restaurant and the menu options are decidedly not eating disorder-approved.

Looking over the menu, you see a food you want and decide to challenge yourself to eat the mac and cheese, normally a terrifying prospect. Everyone orders, including the woman you don't care for.

She orders a salad, boisterously pointing out she's "eating clean" and smirking a bit when you order the macaroni and cheese. She makes a snide remark, something along the lines of, "I guess you're taking the night off from healthy eating." Instantly, your eating disorder chimes in, concurring with her statement. A cacophony of criticism echoes in your head.

Luckily, your best friend is there to stick up for you. Only, this time, she says nothing. Neither does the other woman who's kind but quiet. She doesn't seem like the type to tell someone to speak kindly. Dinner carries on. You try to enjoy the food while the obnoxious woman drones on at the table complaining about how she doesn't make enough money, saying how she hates dating and moaning about all the things she's trying to do to lose weight.

Without self-as-context, you see this situation through the eating disorder's perspective; your eating disorder has you feeling anxious, pulls you away from enjoying the food, and supports the woman's criticism of you. From your eating disorder's perspective, you should listen to her. Her opinion should matter. And, your eating disorder isn't going to ignore how your friend didn't come to your defense.

If you use self-as-context to watch this episode, however, you see it from a different angle. You see it more objectively and less emotionally. Here, you picture yourself stepping out of your body and watching the scene go by, kind of like people-watching at the airport—only, this time, you're one of the people being watched.

Self-as-context not only allows you to separate from triggering feelings, it also allows you to sit back and gather data on the people around you. Your observing self objectively notices how people are treating you and how they treat each other, the same as when you watch a TV show. You notice which characters like each other, which get along, and which ones shouldn't spend time together.

When you lose perspective and your eating disorder blocks you from seeing things from your observing self's point of view, you're more likely to feel triggered. Sometimes, this loss of perspective makes it difficult for you to notice what you need to regarding other people, specifically how they treat you and other people they're around, all of which is valuable data.

Treatment

YOU CAN USE self-as-context to help get you through some of the more difficult parts of treatment as well. This can be especially helpful when you are doing an activity involving food such as eating a fear food in a therapy session or eating a meal with your therapy group. For our example, let's use eating a fear food with one of your treatment providers, such as your therapist or dietitian.

Imagine whatever food you find scary or triggering. Sometimes people with eating disorders really like a particular food but their eating disorder has turned it into a binge food, interfering with having a peaceful relationship with that food.

Got that food in mind? Okay, now, set the stage. You go

to the provider's office. You brought the food with you in the bag. The two of you plan to eat it together and process through the feelings as they come up.

As you begin to eat the food, bite by bite, you feel the discomfort rise. It's challenging. This food was banned by your eating disorder for so long. You feel anxious and uncomfortable. Feelings of regret start to rise up as your eating disorder whispers in your ear, "See, this was a bad idea. You can't do this."

Using the observing self, you can watch this as an episode. What I see in this episode is the main character, you, being very brave. Eating trigger foods can feel awful, especially when you're beginning to practice eating them. You can see the eating disorder as a character in the episode too; picture it sitting on your shoulder, speaking unhelpful, disempowering, discouraging things to you.

Another great opportunity to use the observing self perspective arises when you have treatment appointments that you, or rather, your eating disorder doesn't want to attend. If you're doing any kind of meaningful work in therapy, nutrition appointments, or treatment, inevitably you will have times when you don't want to go. The eating disorder can take advantage of this by emphasizing the inconveniences and obstacles of attending.

Your eating disorder might direct your focus to traffic on the way to the appointment and all the other people on the road driving terribly. It might draw your attention to the other people in your treatment program that you don't like, making you focus on all the ways they annoy you.

As this happens, you can take a step back mentally, sitting in the observing self perspective. You'll notice, viewing this as an episode, that lots of stressful things are going on around you; traffic, other people annoying you, to name only a few. However, from the observing self perspective, seeing things as self-in-context, you see these things as happening around you. You are not hooked on the stress. You are not tied to the eating disorder's complaints and grumblings, all of which ultimately try to dissuade you from engaging in treatment.

Instead of feeling bound to the discomfort, you know you have that part of you, the observing self, to help you see things from a distance. Seeing difficult moments in treatment from a distance can help when your eating disorder is trying to get you to give up.

The Takeaway

WHEN YOU HAVE AN EATING DISORDER, it causes you to lose perspective and to see things instead from its point of view. Self-as-context is the opposite of that. One way to think of self-as-context is to think of it as your observing self. Your observing self is the part of you that can mentally step out of a situation and watch it unfold, like watching an episode of TV.

Self-as-context is helpful because it offers you a place of solace when things feel difficult; you can always move into the director/observer role when you need distance from a situation. Self-as-context is a skill that helps you to see things objectively and maybe even reduce the power of triggers.

25

UNCLEAR VALUES
DEFINED VALUES

Values are the principles that guide your life and lead you to be the kind of person you want to be in the world. ACT aims to increase clarity of values and as well as to increase action that supports living your values. Examples of values include kindness, bravery, freedom, curiosity, and honesty.

Values are important because they're the ideals you work toward, the things that inform how you should act and what you need to do. If you value courage and you are faced with the choice to accept a challenge or to remain comfortable, living life in accordance with your values tells you to take the risk.

With an eating disorder, values become muddled. The values of your eating disorder override the values of your authentic self. Your eating disorder has its own value set. It often values self-interest, vanity, security, approval, competition, and comfort. If you ask anyone who is recovered, they'll tell you the values they live as a recovered person are different from those they moved toward while their eating disorder was present. Living life in accordance with your authentic self's values—following *your values*, not your eating disorder's— ultimately results in recovery.

It's important to note that values are not the same as goals. Goals are destinations whereas values are the direction you travel. Goals are end points that *can be* attained. Values, however, *cannot* be attained. Instead, values can be lived in each moment. Values are what we stand for, not a final destination.

Consider painting as an examples of goals versus values. You may have a goal to paint something beautiful for your home. You can break this down into smaller goals such as learning about the tools you need, learning basic painting techniques and becoming advanced enough in painting to create art to hang in your home. The goal of painting something for your home has an end.

When we consider values associated with painting, you may value beauty, creativity and the pleasure of the process of making art. Creativity has no end. Beauty has no end. Pleasure has no end. All those values, however, give you direction as you move toward your goals; they direct you to actually paint.

Spoiler alert: your eating disorder has very different values than your authentic, healthy self.

In the following sections, we'll explore how your eating disorder clouds you from being able to see your true values and discuss some of the potential values your eating disorder most likely holds.

Food

EATING disorders directly interfere with your authentic values about food. If you ask most people who've never had an eating disorder or people who have recovered from one, what their values are regarding food, they are likely to say nourishment and pleasure.

Valuing nourishment means you consider how food supports your body in completing all the amazing functions it performs for you over and over every single day. Valuing nourishment means that when you consider your food choices overall, the nutrition they provide is part of the equation. You see food as a resource to support your body, and therefore, yourself.

Valuing pleasure from food means you think food should also bring you enjoyment. Valuing nourishment alone means you could eat only things that are highly nutrient dense, completely disregarding how they taste. If you only care about nourishment, or about the nutritional side of food, eating becomes a joyless, utilitarian chore. At the other extreme, valuing pleasure alone means you disregard your body's need for nourishment in favor of eating things solely for them being tasty.

You get to determine what your values around food are. I can't decide that for you. However, I will say that in my own recovery journey and in my work with clients, I've seen balancing pleasure and nourishment heal people's relationship with food.

On the restricting-food rules side of the continuum, your eating disorder tries to sway you toward valuing foods only for their stats: how few calories they have, how "clean" they are, what food group they belong to, etc. This is another iteration of your eating disorder using food rules. Here, however, the food rules have become so habitual and commonplace, you've lost sight of your original value of nourishment.

When you value nourishment from the point of view of

your authentic self, you see foods for all they bring to the table. You see the ways they support your body, strengthen it, and fuel your life. When you value nourishment, you trust that choosing what veggie to eat with dinner isn't the end of the world. If you feel like having spinach but your eating disorder tells you kale is better, valuing nourishment lets you know that both foods contribute lovingly to your body.

When you value pleasure, you can choose spinach over kale because you think it will be more enjoyable to eat that particular night. Valuing pleasure in food is important because it elevates eating food from being a burden, to being something potentially delightful. Experiencing pleasure from food is normal and good.

Your eating disorder muddies the waters by either completely disconnecting you from pleasure—telling you that experiencing pleasure from food is bad and shameful— or by making pleasure your only consideration with food, disregarding what your body is asking for in terms of nourishment.

Your eating disorder can also take up so much space in your life that food becomes the only or the primary means for you to experience pleasure. Having a healthy variety of pleasurable activities is critical for recovery. Food can be one component of pleasure but becomes problematic when it's the only means. You can also experience pleasure from spending time with friends, or dancing, or being creative, or any number of other things. Having options means you don't have to turn to food for everything.

Consider this: if you didn't have an eating disorder, what values would you have around food? What would your values about nourishment and pleasure look like?

Self

YOUR EATING DISORDER twists your values about yourself. Primarily, it does this to get you off track, to distract you by making food the issue again, and to disempower you. Figuring out what your values are can be tricky.

The question, "What do you value?" feels too broad to me. Let's narrow it. Another way I've heard of asking the question is by asking "What do you want to be about?" Great question. What do *you* want to be about? Your answer will inform your values about yourself.

So, what do you want to be about, really? Maybe you want to be about fun and love and charity and learning, and about exploration and taking risks. If you're truly honest with yourself, holding nothing back, is your eating disorder helping you to live in line with these values? Would it be easier to follow your authentic values without your eating disorder?

Absolutely.

Sometimes, eating disorders seem like they support you living a values-driven life but they don't. Ultimately, your eating disorder cares about the value set it brings to your life. Eating disorders commonly value approval over risk taking, attractiveness over self-care, and achievement over authenticity.

Eating disorders can steer you so far away from your values that you wind up acting selfishly or constantly worrying about your appearance. Those things get in the way of you fully experiencing life, connecting with others, contributing to the world, and learning and growing.

It's also not uncommon for your eating disorder to make weight the most important value. You aced a test? Doesn't matter because you still weigh [X] pounds. You're a loving, kind person? No one cares because you're fat. You just won an award at work? It's meaningless because you're not thin enough.

Valuing thinness, or really any particular body shape, is a distraction from focusing on your true values. When you live your authentic values, you'll find there isn't room left over for the minor things your eating disorder routinely gets worked up about.

Others

EATING disorders cloud the values people have about their relationships with others. Your eating disorder's primary value with regard to other people is competition. Specifically, it values winning.

Your eating disorder doesn't care about genuinely connecting with other people. It cares about being better than they are. It cares about being thinner and smarter and prettier and more accomplished than anyone around. If you find yourself relating to this, please be gentle with yourself. There's no need to feel ashamed. This is how eating disorders work.

One of my clients told me a story about a woman she worked with. She said she hated her coworker. She hated that all their other coworkers seemed to love this woman. She hated when the coworker was successful. She, or rather her eating disorder, especially hated that her coworker was beautiful and thin.

My client talked about wanting to "beat" her coworker at all these things because she felt deeply jealous. One day, during a teambuilding activity, her coworker confessed that she really liked my client and wanted to be friends. She even went as far as to say that sometimes she felt self-conscious around my client, like she couldn't quite measure up.

My client was floored. Her eating disorder had twisted her up in quiet mental competition with her coworker, preventing a friendship that likely would have blossomed much earlier had the eating disorder not been in the way. Moreover, her coworker alluded to the fact that she could sense the competitiveness in my client; it's true, people can sense when you're competing with them and they certainly feel it when you're rooting for them to lose.

In the eating disorder's quest for superiority, it disrupts your relationships. It can damage existing relationships or prevent new ones from forming. Sometimes, people grow tired of sensing they're being judged (by your eating disorder, not the authentic you) and feeling as though they need to compete, and they discontinue the relationship.

Your eating disorder is doing this because the constant competition fuels eating disorder behaviors. Every time you don't measure up, you're triggered to use behaviors. Interfering with your relationships also blocks the love and support you can receive, which can make all the difference in recovery.

Consider how different your relationships would look if you did not have your eating disorder. Would you be more relaxed? More open and less likely to judge? Would it be easier to see other people's strengths if you knew they didn't threaten your own?

Treatment

KNOWING YOUR VALUES, and acting in line with them, is powerful. It enables you to be the person you want to be.

During treatment, you're presented with multiple opportunities to discover and act on your authentic values. Your eating disorder is going to do everything possible to interfere.

Your eating disorder is terrified you'll start treatment and learn how to live as your authentic self. When you're acting from your authentic self, living your values, you are empowered, hopeful, and brave; you feel satisfied deep down in your bones, with who you are. Satisfaction with yourself is antithetical to what your eating disorder needs to thrive. The eating disorder is going to step in the way of your progress.

There are many moment-by-moment examples of how your eating disorder can distort your values in treatment. We can summarize the overall theme of how it does this by saying the eating disorder will always choose comfort over courage. It wants you to remain stuck, afraid, shrinking from challenge, avoiding difficult experiences you need to pass through to recover.

The idea of courage and comfort comes from Brené Brown, Ph.D.'s work. Dr. Brown states that, "We can choose courage or we can choose comfort but we cannot choose both."[9] Your eating disorder exploits this truth. And it always chooses comfort.

Comfort is good, sure, but if we are always comfortable we are not growing. Recovery is a growth process. All the other values you have from your authentic self facilitate recovery as well. Kindness, learning, freedom, joy, fun; all these guide you to making recovery-orientated choices instead of staying stuck in the same familiar misery of the eating disorder.

Think about how you can leverage your values in treatment. How can you use those things as assets in recovery?

What would happen if you allowed your authentic values to guide you rather than the other values your eating disorder holds? What would life look like if you didn't allow your eating disorder to choose comfort over courage for you?

The Takeaway

YOU HAVE different values than your eating disorder. Your eating disorder will always prioritize weight, competition, and comfort over growth, bravery, and acceptance. Your eating disorder clouds your ability to clearly see your values because it doesn't want you living them out.

Knowing and living your values directly threatens your eating disorder. Living life from a place of authenticity in accordance with your values bring joy, meaning, and fulfillment that your eating disorder cannot offer.

26

INACTION AND AVOIDANCE

COMMITTED ACTION

Complementary to clearly understanding your values is committed action. ACT helps people to increase committed action in their lives. With committed action, you're doing things that move you toward living your values, toward being the kind of person you want to be in the world. Your behavior reflects your values. For example, if you value being of service to others, committed action could look like you signing up for a volunteer organization or doing something helpful for another person.

Eating disorders drive you away from committed action. Instead, eating disorders breed inaction. Inaction is when we don't set goals or don't take any steps toward our identified values. Inaction can look like never taking any action at all or procrastinating in taking steps toward your values. Alternatively, we can express inaction through impulsivity by haphazardly pursuing things that do not serve us or that are not recovery-focused, and going in the opposite direction.

Your eating disorder uses inaction to keep you stuck. Sometimes, this can look like your eating disorder delaying you seeking help for it or refusing to do the things necessary for recovery at all. A client I worked with wrote this about inaction:

> *Waiting for tomorrow, day after day, is my go-to inaction. One lapse in perfect eating and there goes my whole day. Instead of making the slightly hard, more productive choice, I give in [to behaviors] and count on tomorrow. Turns out the next day's plan has extended into a year.*

Through inaction, your eating disorder capitalizes on the human tendency to have a difficult time starting a task. It's hard to get moving in recovery. It's hard to pick up the phone to call a new therapist. It's hard to eat meals mindfully instead of bingeing or restricting. It's hard to reach out to others, to share that you're struggling, and to ask for them to support you through it.

Your eating disorder is counting on this. It wants you to delay all actions that move you closer to your values and recovery. Inaction keeps you stuck in the eating disorder.

Food

YOUR EATING DISORDER uses inaction to keep you using behaviors instead of strategies—like mindful eating—that facilitate recovery. This blocks you from living in line with values such as bravery, recovery, and health. For example, you may need to eat a larger quantity of food or a wider variety of foods for your recovery. Your eating disorder has whittled your list of acceptable foods down so severely that you can no longer eat with pleasure and nourishment in mind. However, when you prepare your meal and sit down to eat it, noticing all the foods that aren't allowed, you can't bring yourself to take a bite. This is inaction in action.

Another former client wrote this about inaction with food:

> *I plan to take action against my eating disorder, but in times of stress, I end up hiding behind my old behaviors and reverting back to my old patterns. I tell myself I'll try again tomorrow. And tomorrow becomes the next day and the next day and the next day, and I find myself in a cycle of inaction.*

Inaction isn't just avoiding taking action or delaying. Inaction includes doing things that conflict with living your values. In that example, my client values recovery; she wants it to guide her behavior. However, her eating disorder causes her to use behaviors, which leads her further away from her value of recovery.

Eating disorders use inaction with food to cause you to avoid the uncomfortable yet necessary work you need to do with food itself. Ever put off adding a new food into your meal plan? Have you ever avoided trying out a fear food? Have you ever made excuses to avoid eating out with other people? These are all examples of your eating disorder using inaction to keep you from moving forward in recovery.

It's fairly easy to recognize how eating disorders use inaction to cause restricting, but eating disorders use inaction with bingeing and purging too. Let's talk about inaction and bingeing. One of the key things we work on in treatment for binge eating is slowing down the binge eating process so that people have more awareness of when that behavior is happening. When you have awareness, your ability to interrupt the binge increases. When you're truly aware of your patterns, you can choose if you want to act on them or not.

In therapy, you might be assigned homework to do a mindful check-in with yourself before eating a meal. Checking in with yourself allows you to gauge your levels of hunger and fullness, as well as your desire to binge. But your eating disorder doesn't want you to do the mindful check-in. Your eating disorder would much rather have you set up to binge.

Your eating disorder will make up excuses to avoid mindful check-ins. It might convince you that you don't have time to check in before a meal, or might tell you that you don't like mindfulness, that it's a crock. It could come up with any number of reasons but the result is the same every time; you avoid doing things differently. You're stuck in inaction.

Similarly, with purging, your eating disorder is going to discourage you from taking any steps toward change. To help you stop purging, your therapist might assign you homework to decorate your bathroom with things that remind you of recovery—art work, quotes about recovery, trinkets reminding you of your values.

The eating disorder doesn't want you to change anything. You notice you don't make time to go to the store to get craft supplies to make your recovery decorations. You don't bring any of your treasured knick-knacks that would remind you of recovery into the bathroom. You leave them where they are now. Lo and behold, your bathroom stays the same. And you stay in the same stuck place in the eating disorder.

Eating disorders love to use inaction, especially with food because food is where the proverbial rubber meets the road in recovery. If you don't change what you're doing with food, you can't recover. Your eating disorder will dissuade you from taking any steps toward change with food, making you procrastinate, avoid, and keep everything exactly as it is. If you value recovery or your health, you will have to do the hard work of changing your relationship with food.

Self

INACTION REGARDING your self is when your eating disorder prevents or delays you from working on your personal development. Or, inaction can take the form of you doing things that completely oppose your values.

Eating disorders often make people avoid self-exploration in therapy. I can't tell you how many clients I've worked with who've told me they're afraid to find out who they are without their eating disorder. They're fearful of what they'll find when the eating disorder no longer takes over all their thoughts and actions.

Here's the thing though—that's the good stuff. What's under the eating disorder is the good stuff. *You* are under the eating disorder. Your authentic self buried underneath the eating disorder is amazing. I promise.

Your eating disorder doesn't want you to get down to that layer of authenticity. If you set the eating disorder aside and dig deep, you might find you're strong and interesting, and dreaming of so much more than the eating disorder can ever offer you. Your eating disorder doesn't want you dreaming big, hoping with all your heart, or trusting in your strength and resilience.

Most of the time, clients have a hard time bringing up this deeper work in therapy. Their eating disorders keep them focused on the crises of the day instead. It's not that current events don't matter but sometimes working on crisis after crisis in therapy is a form of avoidance of deeper work.

Eating disorders also interfere with committed action by making you act in ways that are the opposite of your values. One of the primary ways I've seen this happen with my clients, and of the ways it happened with me as well, is in valuing appearance much more than you would if you didn't have an eating disorder.

When I was struggling with my eating disorder, I thought about my appearance, specifically my weight, all the time. Not only was it exhausting and primed me to restrict, but it steered me away from my actual values about appearance. My authentic, healthy self enjoys feeling beautiful, and I do feel beautiful. My authentic self's view of beauty is inclusive and broad, incorporating diversity into what I find beautiful.

My eating disorder, on the other hand, had an extremely narrow definition of beauty. It was a beauty involving being very thin and requiring all other aspects of my appearance to be "perfect". Obsessing over my appearance and having a narrow view of beauty is not how I authentically feel. It is not my true value.

But, my eating disorder successfully wasted a lot of my time and heart on that nonsense. And the avoidance of discovering my real values around appearance kept me focused on perfecting my body, punishing it when it didn't live up to my eating disorder's standards.

Whether the eating disorder is causing you to avoid looking at yourself or to act out of line with your values, its end goal is always to keep you stuck. Avoidance and inaction keep the eating disorder going.

Others

YOUR EATING DISORDER uses inaction in your relationships with others to try to decrease the quality of the relationships. My hunch is that you value relationships, and value having relationships of quality, full of honesty, connection, intimacy, and joy. When relationships are satisfying, all parties involved are honest with each other, able to address and work through conflict, and willing to *do* the things the relationships need in order to be fruitful.

Eating disorders cause people to avoid all kinds of things in relationships. One of the first things eating disorders cause you to avoid is reaching out in the first place. Eating disorders create isolation. It's common for people who have eating disorders to feel anxious about being around others, and about eating in front of them. Your eating disorder doesn't want you to take that first step of calling someone, of scheduling something, or of meeting up with them.

Eating disorders love to make people avoid vulnerability and intimacy. Your eating disorder might allow you to go out with others or talk with friends or family but not tell them about what's really going on for you. Eating disorders don't like it when you share that you're struggling. When you tell someone who cares about you that you're struggling, they want to support you. Your eating disorder doesn't want you to have support. It wants you to keep using behaviors instead, thus preventing you from living your value of deep, satisfying relationships.

Avoidance of intimacy, vulnerability, and asking for help are common among people with eating disorders. Likewise, avoidance of conflict is extremely common too. As we've talked about earlier in this book, conflict in relationships is completely unavoidable and something everyone faces. In fact, effectively working through conflict with another person brings us closer.

Your eating disorder doesn't like the sound of any of that. Your eating disorder would prefer it if you never brought up your needs or concerns with that person. It's much better for your eating disorder if you secretly resent them or feel upset and helpless because you're not getting what you want. You're much more likely to continue using eating disorder behaviors when you're feeling resentful toward the other person or when you're worrying about whether they're mad at you but you avoid bringing it up.

Inaction and avoidance in relationships keep the eating disorder going by fueling you with feelings of loneliness, disconnection, frustration, and dissatisfaction with not getting your needs met. Inaction and avoidance directly step in the way of you getting what you value out of relationships.

Treatment

IF YOUR AUTHENTIC self values health, your eating disorder will get in the way of you doing things for your health. Your eating disorder uses inaction by preventing you from seeking treatment in the first place. This can take many forms. It can look like you're putting off calling a therapist, as one example. Inaction when it comes to starting treatment is extremely powerful. Your eating disorder cuts you off before you can even give treatment a chance, blocking you from acting in line with your value of being healthy.

Treatment is always going to seem scarier when you haven't done it yet. Your eating disorder is counting on you avoiding treatment by avoiding your fear of the unknown, endlessly delaying your progress. It's in your eating disorder's best interest for you to avoid pushing through the fear of getting started.

If you're already in therapy, inaction can also show up by delaying scheduling an intake for a higher level of care after your therapist has mentioned it for weeks. Inaction can also mean not showing up to your intake appointment at a treatment center. It can look like you holding back and not bringing up the concerns you have at the annual visit to your primary care provider. It can even look like missing your first scheduled appointment with a therapist or dietitian. And, of course, inaction can look like people walking out of treatment immediately after they walk in the doors. I've actually heard all these from my clients.

Treatment, no matter what level of care you're at, is where change happens. Treatment is where you have to do the actual day-to-day work of getting the eating disorder out of your life. Inaction helps your eating disorder to directly block recovery by preventing you from taking on the smaller tasks that build toward overall recovery.

Inaction will stop you from going to the grocery store to buy the foods you'll need for the week. Inaction will make you procrastinate in eating a challenging food. Inaction will prevent you from joining a therapy group that would be extremely helpful. And, inaction will cause you to do things contrary to recovery, like walking out of a treatment center, quitting therapy, and using behaviors immediately after therapy sessions.

Anytime you notice you're putting off or not doing something that will move you forward in your recovery, you know this is the eating disorder keeping you stuck with inaction and avoidance.

.

The Takeaway

INACTION INCLUDES ALL behaviors that delay, are contrary to, or completely prevent recovery. Inaction is the stuck-ness eating disorders create. Inaction is the opposite of committed action, which is essential for living authentically, based on your values. Your eating disorder uses inaction in treatment—literally preventing you from doing the work of recovery—as a way of keeping itself going. Taking action toward your values threatens the eating disorder's existence. I highly encourage it!

PART V

Concluding Thoughts and Hope for the Journey

27

CONCLUDING THOUGHTS AND HOPE FOR THE JOURNEY

This book has walked you through all the major concepts from CBT, DBT, and ACT. We've reviewed how the eating disorder distorts your thoughts using All-or-None Thinking, Overgeneralization, and Personalization. We've seen how the eating disorder discounts the positive, focuses you only on the negative, and catastrophizes. It emotionally reasons and *shoulds* all over you with oppressive should statements.

The cognitive distortions caused by the eating disorder keep you stuck, forcing you to see things from the eating disorder's point of view rather than your own. The eating disorder impairs your ability to be mindful, to regulate your emotions, to tolerate difficult emotions or situations, and sets you up to act in unhealthy ways in your relationships. The eating disorder uses all these things to upset you, disempower you, and keep you stuck in the cycle of using the eating disorder to solve all your problems and ease painful feelings.

The section on ACT showed how the eating disorder fuses with your thoughts, making you feel like thoughts produced by the eating disorder are actually your own. But you and your eating disorder are not the same! You learned how the eating disorder wants you to avoid experiences, stuck in inaction. You learned how the eating disorder disrupts your ability to clearly understand your values and stops you from acting in line with those same values. You learned how the eating disorder makes you ruminate over the past and feel terrified of the future, causing you to completely lose perspective.

When I started writing this book, I wanted to give you an outline of all the ways your eating disorder tries to keep you stuck. I wanted to write the playbook for eating disorders so you would feel empowered when you saw the eating disorder using its tricks. And, so you can choose differently.

This book can't get rid of your eating disorder. Only you can do that. But, I hope you, Reader, have much more information and hope for recovery with the perspective of this book. I hope you're able to connect with your authentic self and see things from that perspective, instead of always looking through the eating disorder's lens.

I encourage you to bring this book with you to therapy. I encourage you to re-read and study it as you need. I challenge you to journal about the sections that resonated with you, and I hope you talk with others about what you've learned here and what you want to keep working on.

Most of all, I dare you to believe you can do this. I dare you to believe that you can get back to your perspective. I dare you believe that you can recover, fully, completely, even in the times when it feels hopeless. I dare you to believe in your own greatness and to show it to the world.

ENDNOTES

1. For more information about CBT, please visit The Beck Institute for Cognitive Behavioral Therapy at www.BeckInstitute.org.

2. For more information and research articles on the efficacy of DBT in clinical populations, please visit www.Behavioraltech.org.

3. For more information, please visit Dr. Marsha Linehan's website at www.Behavioraltech.org.

4. Definition taken from Behavioraltech.org, Dr. Marsha Linehan's website. For more information, visit Behavioraltech.org.

5. Taken from DBT Skills Training Handouts and Worksheets, Second Edition by Marsha Linehan, The Guilford Press; 2 edition (October 21, 2014).

6. Definition taken from BehavioralTech.org by Dr. Marsha Linehan.

7. Definition by Steven Hayes, Ph.D., from the website for ACT, The Association for Contextual Behavioral Science, www.ContextualScience.org. For more information regarding ACT, please visit www.ContextualScience.org.

8. To learn more about vulnerability and connection, reference Brené Brown, Ph.D. Dr. Brown is a researcher and social worker who studies vulnerability. Find her at www.BreneBrown.com.

9. Brené Brown, Ph.D., LMSW, is a researcher and social worker who researches vulnerability, shame, and courage. For more information, visit www.BreneBrown.com or read any of her books. Recommended is *Daring Greatly*.

RECOMMENDED READING AND RESOURCES

More About Dr. Janean Anderson:
www.DrJaneanAnderson.com

Books:

Brown, Brené, Ph.D., LMSW. "Daring Greatly: How the Courage to Be Vulnerable Transforms the Way We Live, Love, Parent, and Lead" (Gotham, 2012)

Costin, Carolyn, M.A., M.Ed., MFT. "The Eating Disorder Sourcebook" (McGraw-Hill, 2007)

Johnston, Anita, Ph.D. "Eating in the Light of the Moon: How Women Can Transform Their Relationship With Food Through Myths" (Gurze Books, 2000)

Schaefer, Jenni. "Life Without Ed: How One Woman Declared Independence from Her Eating Disorder and How You Can Too" (McGraw-Hill, 2003)

Tribole, Evelyn, M.S., R.D., and Resch, Elyse, M.S., R.D. "Intuitive Eating: A Revolutionary Program that Works" (St. Martin's Griffin, 2012)

Websites:
Information on DBT and Dr. Marsha Linehan: www.BehavioralTech.org

Information on CBT and Dr. Judith Beck and Dr. Aaron Beck: www.BeckInstitute.org

Information on ACT and Dr. Steven Hayes: www.ContextualScience.org

Information on eating disorders and treatment resources:
National Eating Disorders Association
www.nationaleatingdisorders.org

ACKNOWLEDGMENTS

There are many people without whom this book never would have been possible. Though this is not, by any means, a comprehensive list of everyone I have to thank, it's a start. I am truly grateful to everyone who has taught me, encouraged me, and mentored me. I love you all.

First, I need to acknowledge my husband, Brady. Brady, your unwavering support made this book possible. From the moment I came home one day and said to you, "I know this is crazy, but I think I need to write a book," something changed. You made me feel this was possible. You didn't think it was far-fetched at all. You have faith in me like no one else ever has. I love you dearly. Your love has made me a better person. You make me brave.

To my kid sis, Kari, I love you to pieces. All of our lives you've been there with me, through the good and the really, *really* bad. I appreciate you, especially all of your prayers, words of encouragement, and supportive listening through all the times I complained when I lost my way or felt out of touch with my faith. Your humor, support, and interest in all of my career pursuits have helped me to keep going when things felt insurmountable.

To Kate Merkle, my marble jar friend. Thank you for being my soul sister, for "getting me," on a level most people can't. Thank you for being someone I can always trust and go to even in my most emotionally broken moments. I admire you as a woman and certainly as a treatment professional. Your insight, brilliance, and expertise have changed my life and my client's lives. I love you, girl.

This book also would not have come to fruition without Dr. Anita Johnston. What most people don't know is that when I started writing this book, the idea of writing a book, let alone getting anyone to read it one day, seemed beyond absurd. Nevertheless, I indulged the absurdity.

As I began writing, I felt more and more alone. I decided to reach out to other authors in the field, hoping to gain wisdom from their experience. After many non-responses, Dr. Johnston replied. And, it seems serendipity helped us to connect.

Anita, thank you for being my mentor. I am honored and humbled every day to have you as a teacher in this work. You are brilliant. You have been more than generous with your time, wisdom, and encouragement. Thank you for believing in me. I hope each day I can make myself a little more like you.

I would also like to thank A.C. Fuller, my "author friend." A.C., thank you for the insights, information, and ongoing encouragement of me with my writing process. Thank you for being an inspiration to me about writing and publishing. I wish you continued career success, including dump trucks full of money and gold-plated bathtubs.

Thank you to my team of Beta Readers for giving me amazing feedback on earlier, less polished drafts of this book. It means the world to me that you took the time to read my work, carefully consider it, and share your thoughts with me. Beta Readers include: Aimee Becker, Aly Pots, Amanda Whitbeck, Coryell Driver, Sarah LeGare, and my husband. You all rock!

Thank you also to my team at Colorado Therapy & Assessment Center, my private practice; Dr. Lauren Millard, Allison Cohan, LCSW, Dr. Megan Wilhite, Dr. Kelsey South, Dr. Saryn Levy, and Dr. Brienne Brown. You are all extraordinary professionals. I feel honored to work with each of you. Thank you for joining me in my wild pursuits including private practice and this book. I am very grateful for each of you.

And, lastly, to my clients and podcast listeners, thank you. Thank you, thank you, thank you! I wish I could hug every one of you. Please know, you are the reason I do all of this. Through working with you in therapy or getting to know you via email from the podcast, your hearts never cease to astonish me with their tenderness and strength. I hold all of you in mine.

OTHER WORKS

Watch Out for the Recover Your Perspective Workbook and Other Books!

Stay in touch with Dr. Anderson:

Newsletter Sign-Up at www.DrJaneanAnderson.com

DrJaneanAnderson.com

Facebook.com/DrAndersonAuthor

Twitter.com/DrJanean

Want more recovery?

Check out The Eating Disorder Recovery Podcast

on Apple Podcasts, YouTube, or at
EatingDisorderRecoveryPodcast.com

ABOUT THE AUTHOR

Dr. Janean Anderson is a licensed psychologist, author, and host of The Eating Disorder Recovery Podcast. She earned her Ph.D. in Counseling Psychology from Colorado State University and completed her predoctoral internship at the University of California, Davis.

Dr. Anderson is a Certified Eating Disorders Specialist (CEDS) through the International Association of Eating Disorder Professionals (IAEDP). Dr. Anderson has specialized in the treatment eating disorders since 2008.

Dr. Anderson is the Founder and Director of Colorado Therapy & Assessment Center, an outpatient treatment center specializing in eating disorders in Denver, Colorado where she resides with her loved ones including her golden retriever.

For more information please visit:
www.DrJaneanAnderson.com